Globalboho AXL agenda.

13 month Go with the flow Lunar edition

OTHER KOKOPELLIMA PRESS BOOKS BY ANGEL BRYNNER

Eutaxis Ecclesia Exodus

Erebus Exist Esthesis Epicharis

Elision Elysum Empyrean

AOLAB Active Art (therapy) decks BY ANGEL BRYNNER

ZION HALCYON DELUGE BLOOD OF MY BLOOD

FLESH OF MY FLESH BONE OF MY BONE

BLACKWATER OVERFLOW EDEN ZENITH

AOLAB Travelogues BY ANGEL BRYNNER

BOTTOM OF THE NINTH WARD BULLETINS BLACKWATER RISING

Anthologies BY ANGEL BRYNNER

FIRESTARTER FIREWALKER

AOLAB Active Art Revisionist books BY ANGEL BRYNNER

(The road to) ZION grievechonic

(The road to) HALCYON grievechronic

(The road to) DELUGE grievechronic

(The road to) BLOOD grievechronic

Globalboho AXL

13 month Go with the flow Lunar edition

agenda.

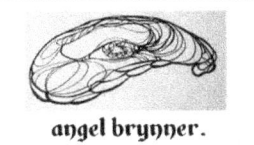
angel brynner.

KOKOPELLIMA PRESS

Copyright 2023 by Angel Brynner

All Rights Reserved

Printed in the United States

Kokopellima Press. www.kokopellimapress.com

Cataloging-in-Publication Data

Brynner, Angel

Globalboho AXL Agenda | 13 month go with the flow Lunar edition

Hardcover ISBN: 978-1-950077-82-3

This is a work of non-fiction. No part of This publication may be reproduced or transmitted in any form or by an means, electronic or mechanical, including photocopying, recording, NFT or any other information storage and retrieval system, without written permission of the Publisher.

Cover artwork and book design:

AOLAB/AngelBrynner.

Additional image credit:freepik,pexels.

Website: http://www.angelbrynner.com

If found, there is a reward.
Name:
Email:

Let's get into IT.

"As always...It's good to have a personal agenda."

The M.O. Here
is very simple:

USE Everything you've got
to get where you want with integrity
so you can look you in the Eye once
you get there.
&
See who you really are now so you can
effectively design who
you aim to grow into.

Globalboho Geist

An explanation of the Globalboho revisionist agenda protocol to help you get your sea legs.

A perfect place to begin.

INSTRUCTIONS:

Geist, Gnosis, then
SECTION ground Zero: futureshock, freewrites, repositories & depositories:

Our future is embedded in our now.
Alvin Toffler\ Futureshock.

This "overview of you" section is the warm-up, where you start doing the work. Think about the year in front of you in broad strokes, as if your dreams were truly possible. Free-write it out... then take the time to expand on the ideas that rise up.

Play *with* your pending life like it can be fn amazing.

You get a few variations on the "quarter theme" to get your envisioning juices flowing + space for keeping track of quotes you run into out on the road going for yours, a triggers spread to begin building out your own inner arsenal to help you navigate around them, and logs for the littlest seedling dreams that you may not have even watered yet, but know you have on your heart.

SECTION ONE: Seasonal M.O.

The "get to know who TF you are & who TF you'd like to be this new season" section.-

Have fun with it. HAVE THE COURAGE TO IMAGINE YOUR IDEAL SEASON WITH NO HOLDS BARRED & no outside input.

This is a haptic conversation/log between You & Higher You(& whoever you pray to when the shit hits the fan to get you out of it).

Daydream it,
Define it,
Design it...
then try it on for size.

You get 4 of these sections. 4 quarter.

SECTION TWO: Monthly M.O.'s

This Monthly section is where the rubber really hits the road. You will win(or reset so you can win) Here.

This ain't yo momma's filofax monthly calendar*-We're not weighing you down with the day by day way of yore because when it comes to real change
there are some things you gotta shore up first and load in to your body, mind and behavioral patterns to go new places. & You need to be able to breathe while learning how to do that without beating yourself up on the road to better because you missed a day.

Once you get planning your month out and walking it out down, those ideal days with room to go hardcore[GB Revisionist] or free write flow forward [GB AOLAB] will be a breeze with no condemnation slowing you down.

Consider the GB AWOL agenda the mountain you consciously climb & learn to make your own Clouds on to create the latter rains you dream of dancing in.

This isn't magic, per se.
It's science lab mode, variations on Circadian rhythms & keying into earthly cycles that life already flows to, to get you where you want to go.

You get 13 monthly sections.
[+ 1 extra in the back to keep it going until your next agenda arrives OR To use as your scratch sheet section to figure out your whathaveyous.]

SECTION ***: a few extras to play with as a gift.

As usual with GB agendas

Give yourself the gold star from jump

& Just do what you think it'd take to deserve it.

Yep. Simply do that sh*t. On repeat.

Instead of the sh*t you keep doing that ain't working.

Globalboho Gnosis

A few info sheets on different holistic roads that may pique your interest on the road to deep diving YOU.

The "good news" is
the world ain't what it used to be.
It's a wilder kind of war out there
Than before...& a little extra
weaponry rocked on the way to
your whathaveyous couldn't hurt.
So...gear up & get out there & win!

Helmet of Salvation/Ephesians 6:17

Breastplate of Righteousness /Ephesians 6:14

Belt of Truth /Ephesians 6:14

Sword of the Spirit /Ephesians 6:17

Shield of Faith/Ephesians 6:16

Feet of Peace/Ephesians 6:15

"& when you've done all
you can think
To do, stand."
- **Ephesians 6:13**

[Dive deeper on your own]

ARMOR of GOD

solfeggio frequencies

- 174 hz / removes pain
- 285 hz / influences energy field
- 369 hz / liberation from guilt & fear
- 417 hz / facilitates change
- 528 hz / repairs DNA (love frequency)
- 639 hz / heals relationships
- 741 hz / awaken intuition
- 852 hz / attracts soul tribe
- 963 hz / connect with light & spirit

Vibe Tribe [Hertz]:

174 **285** **369** **417** **528** **639** **741** **852** **963**

extras:
432 hz / miracle tone of nature

Brain waves:

- THETA 4 to 8 hz / meditation & creativity
- BETA 13 to 35 hz / problem solving
- ALPHA 8 to 13 hz / relaxed reflection
- DELTA 0.5 to 4 hz / deep sleep
- GAMMA 35+ hz / heightened awareness

[Dive deeper on your own]

Hertz Vibe Tribe

Five elements theory is a Chinese philosophy that describes how the fundamental elements in nature flow into & interact with each other.

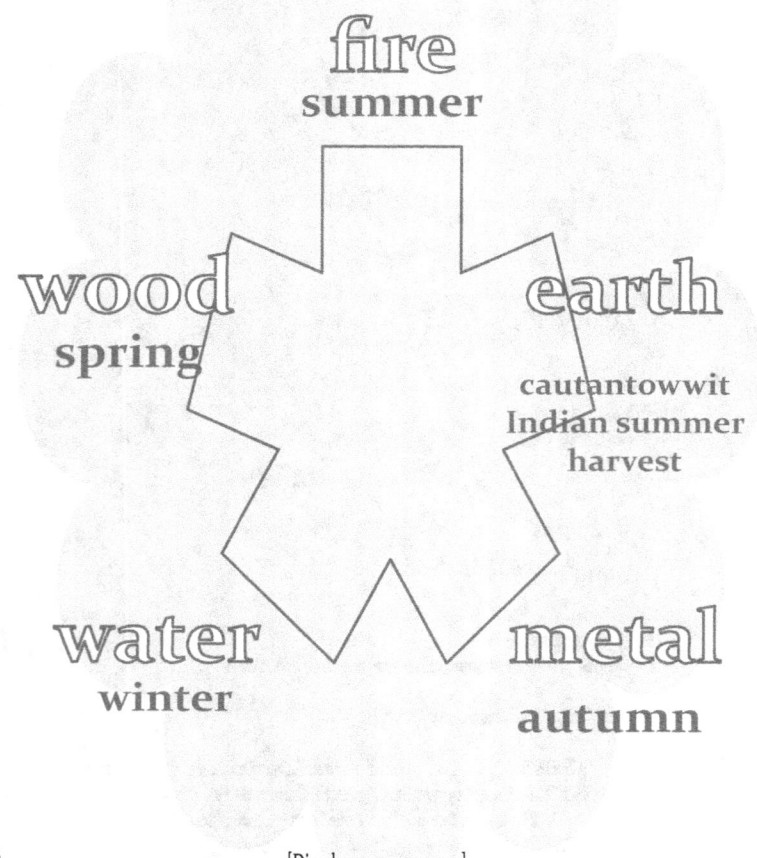

fire
summer

wood
spring

earth
cautantowwit
Indian summer
harvest

water
winter

metal
autumn

[Dive deeper on your own]

The Five Elements

Short & Sweet:

A "Loka"
Is a state of
consciousness
One is interacting
With the world
from, whether
One is aware of
It or not. They sync
With spiritual realms
Above & below ours
In Hinduism.

[Dive deeper on your own]

A "Chakra"
is usually
seen as an
Energy center
That needs to
"be in balance."

The Upper Lokas [Level of Awareness]	location	Deals with / Awareness of:
Satyaloka		illumination
Tapoloka		Divine sight
Janaloka		Divine love
Maharloka		Direct recognition/ Universal unity
Svargaloka		Willpower/Mind over matter
Bhuvarloka		Reason/ Seat of the soul
Bhuloka	earth	Memory/ Time transcendence
The 7 chakras taught in the west:	**Location:**	**Deals with / Awareness of:**
Sahasrara	crown	Inspiration & oneness
Vishuddhi	throat	communication
Anahata	heart	Pure love & compassion
Manipura	Solar plexus	Empowerment free will
Svadhisthana	sacral	Sex, power, creativity, desire, intimacy
Muladhara	root	Grounding & survival
The Lower Lokas [animal instincts/ states of darkness/ Levels of fixation]	**location**	**Deals with/ fixated on**
Atala	hips	Fear & lust
Vitala	thighs	Anger & resentment
Sutala	knees	Jealousy & envy
Talatala	calves	Confusion & doubt
Rasatala	ankles	Selfishness & pride
Mahatala	feet	consciencelessness
Patala	soles	Hatred & malice

The 21 (actual) chakras

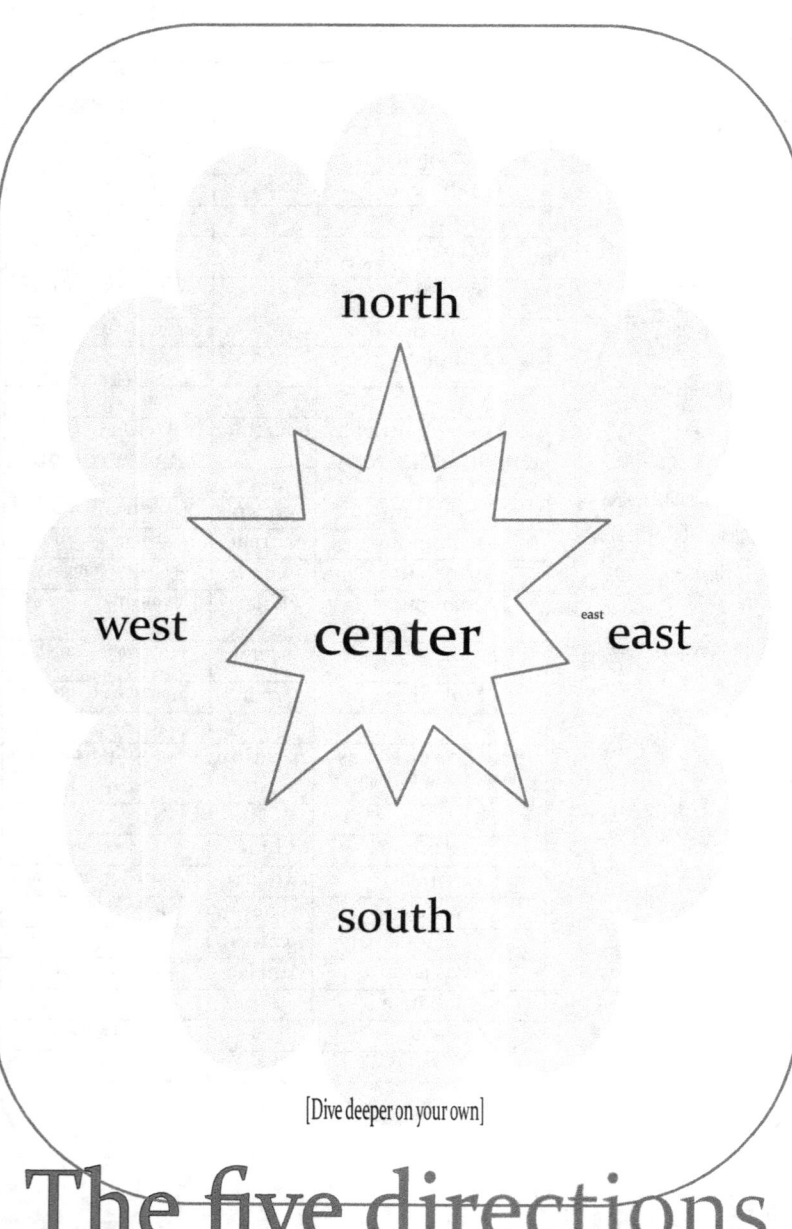

The five directions

According to Trungpa, we don't Wait until we die to enter the BARDO realm that Tibetan Buddhists See as waiting for us Upon death. We dance in & out of the 6 states as we live Our lives. Our Experience of the Present is always Colored by one Of six psychological States.

Freedom From this Madness is Possible.

Dive deeper on your own.

The god realm
[bliss]

The jealous god realm
[jealousy & lust for entertainment]

The human realm
[passion & desire]

The animal realm
[ignorance]

The hungry ghost realm
[poverty & possessiveness]

The hell realm
[aggression & hatred]

Chogyam Trungpa's Bardos

Futureshock Freewrites, Repositories & Depositories.

1st quarter

2nd quarter

| Free Write | | Free Write |

career

| Free Write | | Free Write |

3rd quarter

4th quarter

1st quarter

2nd quarter

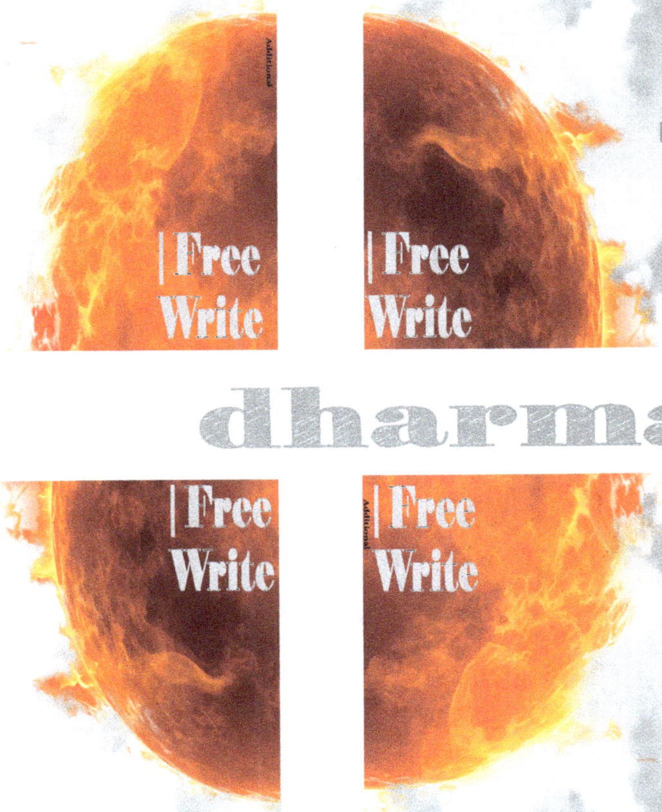

Additional
| Free Write
| Free Write
dharma
| Free Write
Additional
| Free Write

3rd quarter

4th quarter

1st quarter

2nd quarter

Free Write

Free Write

money

Free Write

Free Write

3rd quarter

4th quarter

1st quarter

Additional image credit: freepik

| Free Write

2nd quarter

Free Write

3rd quarter

Free Write

Free Write

4th quarter

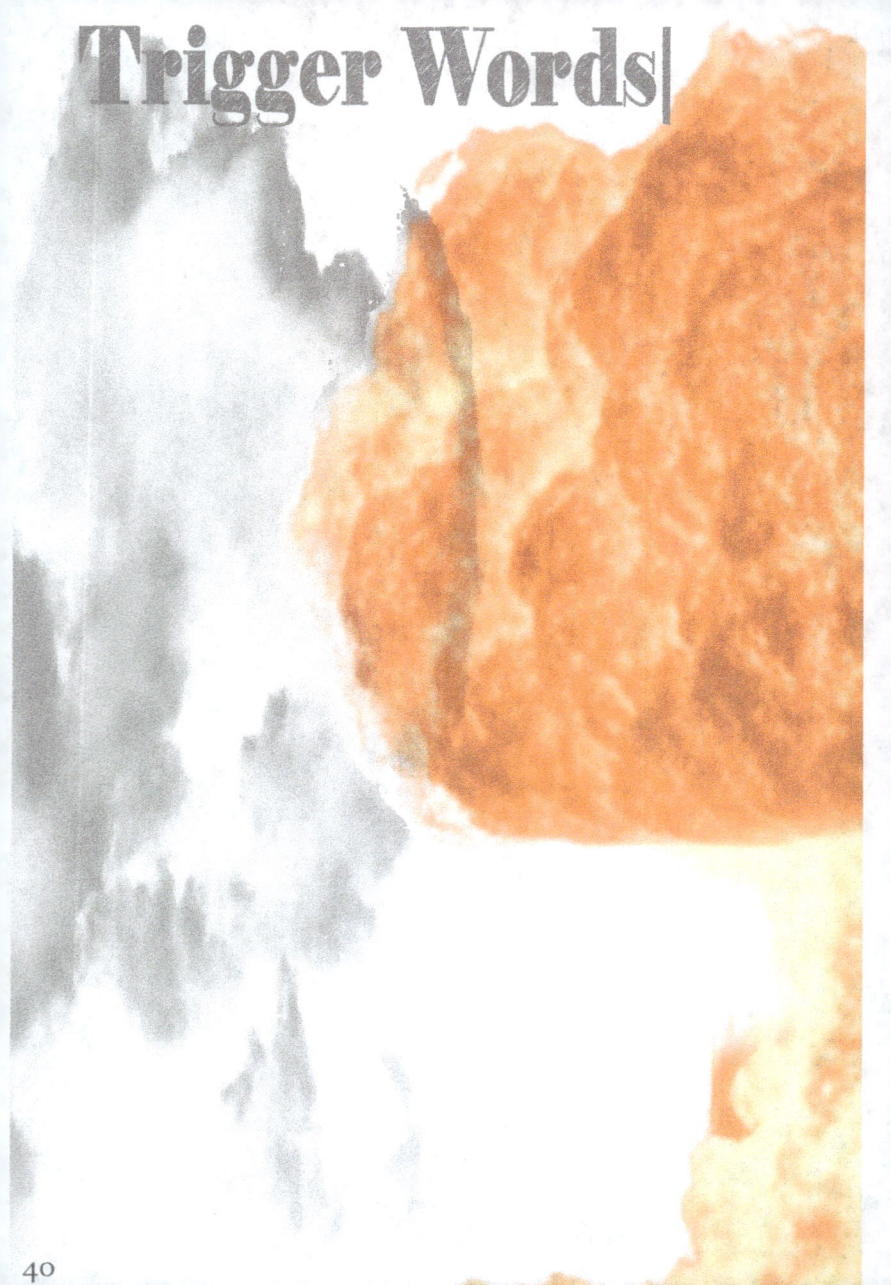

Trigger Words

Free-write

Free Write

Seedlings| Ideas depository

| Free Write

Seedlings|Ideas depository

Quotes| wise words repository

Free Write

Quotes| wise words repository

Seasonal modus operandi

Dream Play/

Who are you at play?

How does it feel (Imagine being that)**?**

What do you smell doing it?

Where are you?

List 2 things you can do this season to bring you in closer alignment to that dream <u>now:</u> (time is a construct)

1

2

Re-read this at DayUP & b4Bed

date	month	
1		
2		
3		
4		
5		
6		
7		
8		
9		
10		
11		
12		
13		
14		
15		
16		
17		
18		
19		
20		
21		
22		
23		
24		
25		
26		
27		
28		
29		
30		
31		

Manifestation log

Dream R& R/
Who are you at rest?

How does it feel (Imagine being that)?

What do you smell doing it?

Where are you?

List 3 things you can do this season to bring you in closer alignment to that dream now: (time is a construct)

1

2

3

Re-read this at DayUP & b4Bed

date	month	
1		
2		
3		
4		
5		
6		
7		
8		
9		
10		
11		
12		
13		
14		
15		
16		
17		
18		
19		
20		
21		
22		
23		
24		
25		
26		
27		
28		
29		
30		
31		

Manifestation log

Dream Job Title/

Who are you at work?

Imagine doing that…How does it feel?

What does it smell like?

Where are you?

List 5 things to do this season to bring you closer to that dream <u>now</u>

1

2

3

4

5

Imagining it is the 2d step after figuring out what your "IT" is~

1		
2		
3		
4		
5		
6		
7		
8		
9		
10		
11		
12		
13		
14		
15		
16		
17		
18		
19		
20		
21		
22		
23		
24		
25		
26		
27		
28		
29		
30		
31		
date	month	

Manifestation log

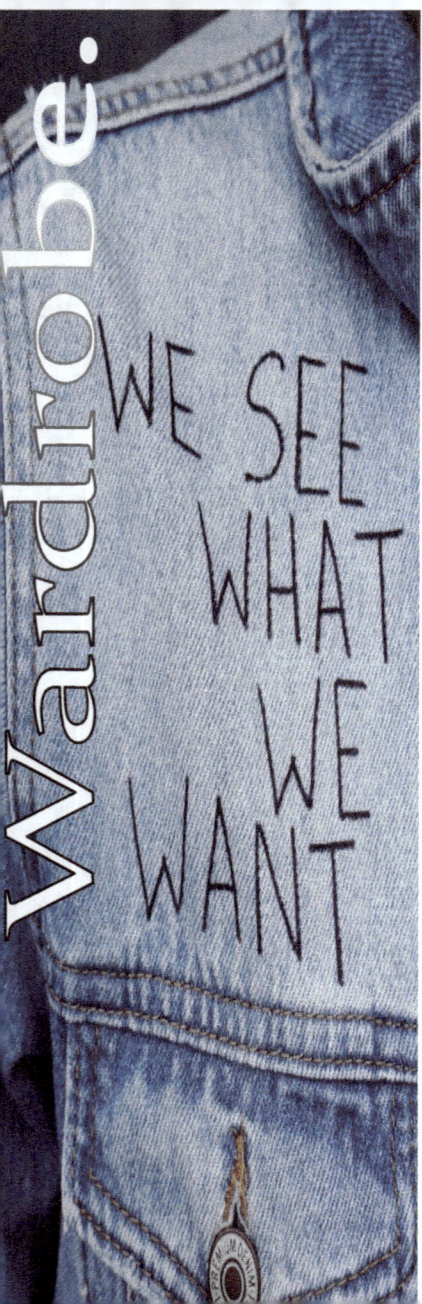

(Dream capsule closet)

How close can you get it?
[Current rotation]

Things needed to bridge
The above gap:

Get…(& rock) at least 1 of
the above items(or similar)
to see how you feel in real time
wearing it..

1.

Seasonal style center

Theme

Color focus

Style spirit animal

Place inspiration

"Clean up nice" trick

New style intel to test

Elevated Off-duty look

Habit to send on sabbatical

The Culling fields:

fuck[with]:　　　　　　marry[into rotation]:

put up[donate]:　　　kill[trash]:　　　　love[repair]:

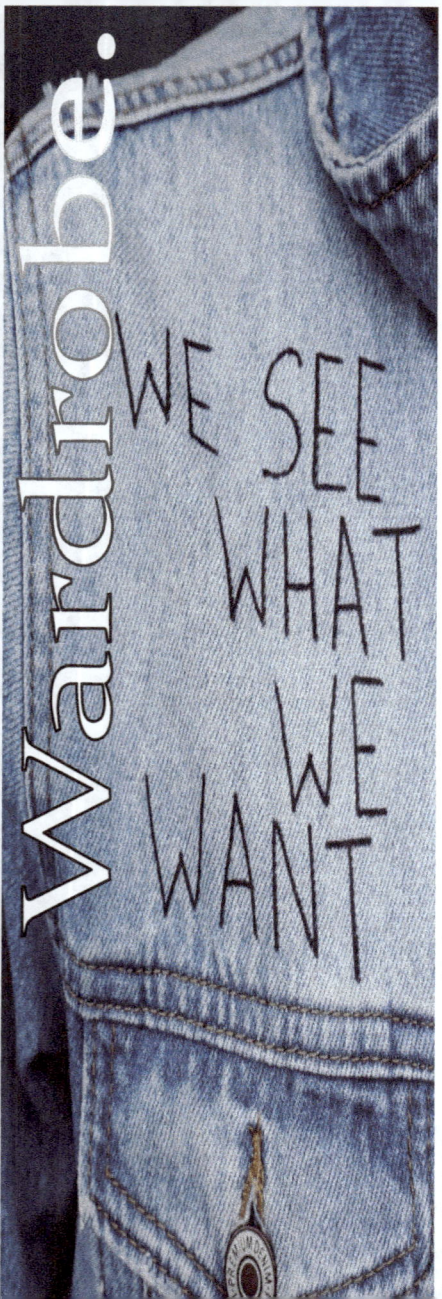

(Dream capsule closet)

How close can you get it?
[Current rotation]

Things needed to bridge
The above gap:

Get...(& rock) at least 1 of
the above items(or similar)
to see how you feel in real time
wearing it..

Seasonal style center

Theme

Color focus

Style spirit animal

Place inspiration

"Clean up nice" trick

New style intel to test

Elevated Off-duty look

Habit to send on sabbatical

The Culling fields:

fuck[with]:

marry[into rotation]:

put up[donate]:

kill[trash]:

love[repair]:

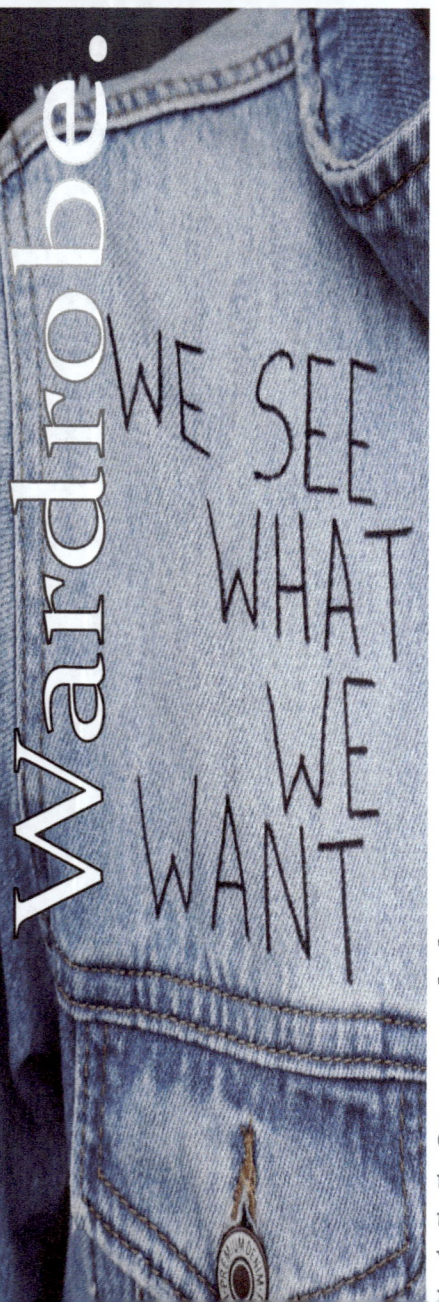

(Dream capsule closet)

How close can you get it?
[Current rotation]

Things needed to bridge
The above gap:

Get...(& rock) at least 1 of
the above items(or similar)
to see how you feel in real time
wearing it..

1.

Seasonal style center

Theme

Color focus

Style spirit animal

Place inspiration

"Clean up nice" trick

New style intel to test

Elevated Off-duty look

Habit to send on sabbatical

The Culling fields:

fuck[with]:

marry[into rotation]:

put up[donate]:

kill[trash]:

love[repair]:

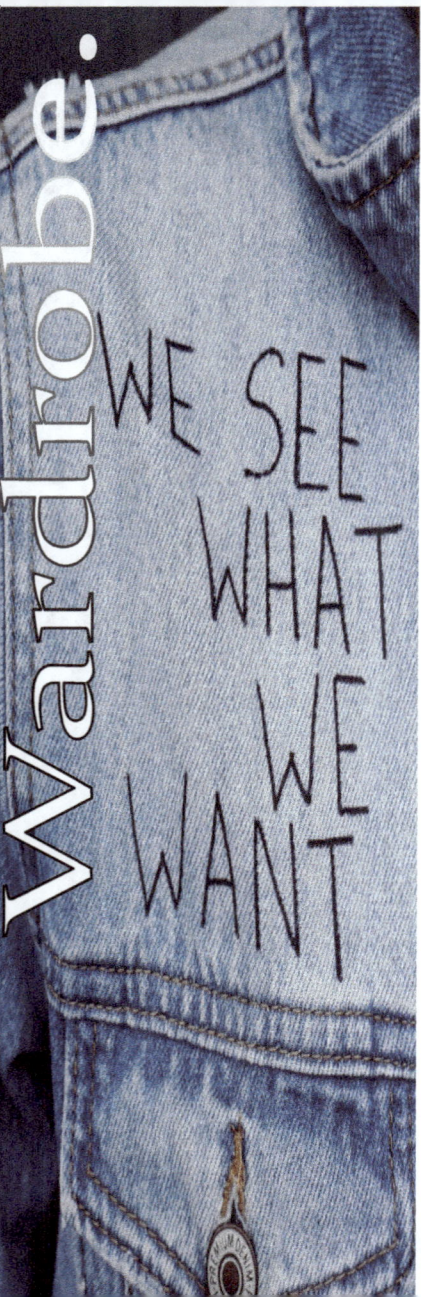

(Dream capsule closet)

How close can you get it?
[Current rotation]

Things needed to bridge
The above gap:

Get...(& rock) at least 1 of
the above items(or similar)
to see how you feel in real time
wearing it..

Seasonal style center

Theme

Color focus

Style spirit animal

Place inspiration

"Clean up nice" trick

New style intel to test

Elevated Off-duty look

Habit to send on sabbatical

The Culling fields:

fuck[with]:   **marry[into rotation]:**

put up[donate]:   **kill[trash]:**   **love[repair]:**

Aesthetics.

date	month	month	month
1			
2			
3			
4			
5			
6			
7			
8			
9			
10			
11			
12			
13			
14			
15			
16			
17			
18			
19			
20			
21			
22			
23			
24			
25			
26			
27			
28			
29			
30			
31			

Seasonal grooming wellness LOG

SIMPLE. Did you do something to care for you today? Y | N

This is simple... A season has about 90 days. This grid gives you 50 days to plan out wellness & grooming things to do to take care of your "ship," your body & soul--whatever you like to call all of it- across a season.

Take care of your Self.
Treat yourself.

Practice Giving a fuck.
For You... LOVE YOU.
First. All else is gravy after you nail that one.

&Log it.

You'll be fine.
It is basically
Doing
Something
Nice to yourself
every other
day. You can
Handle that

Seasonal Wellness /Self-Care BINGO
[what|when]:

69

Aesthetics.

date	month	month	month
1			
2			
3			
4			
5			
6			
7			
8			
9			
10			
11			
12			
13			
14			
15			
16			
17			
18			
19			
20			
21			
22			
23			
24			
25			
26			
27			
28			
29			
30			
31			

Seasonal grooming wellness LOG

SIMPLE. Did you do something to care for you today? Y | N

This is simple... A season has about 90 days. This grid gives you 50 days to plan out wellness & grooming things to do to take care of your "ship," your body & soul--whatever you like to call all of it- across a season.

Take care of your Self.
Treat yourself.

Practice Giving a fuck.
For You... LOVE YOU.
First. All else is gravy after you nail that one.

&Log it.

You'll be fine.
It is basically
Doing
Something
Nice to yourself
every other
day. You can
Handle that

Seasonal Wellness /Self-Care BINGO
[what|when]:

Aesthetics.

date	month	month	month
1			
2			
3			
4			
5			
6			
7			
8			
9			
10			
11			
12			
13			
14			
15			
16			
17			
18			
19			
20			
21			
22			
23			
24			
25			
26			
27			
28			
29			
30			
31			

Seasonal grooming wellness LOG

SIMPLE. Did you do something to care for you today? Y | N

This is simple... A season has about 90 days. This grid gives you 50 days to plan out wellness & grooming things to do to take care of your "ship," your body & soul- -whatever you like to call all of it- across a season.

Take care of your Self.
Treat yourself.

Practice Giving a fuck.
For You... LOVE YOU.
First. All else is gravy after you nail that one.

&Log it.

You'll be fine.
It is basically
Doing
Something
Nice to yourself
every other
day. You can
Handle that

Seasonal Wellness /Self-Care BINGO
[what|when]:

Aesthetics.

date	month	month	month
1			
2			
3			
4			
5			
6			
7			
8			
9			
10			
11			
12			
13			
14			
15			
16			
17			
18			
19			
20			
21			
22			
23			
24			
25			
26			
27			
28			
29			
30			
31			

Seasonal grooming wellness LOG

SIMPLE. Did you do something to care for you today? Y | N

This is simple... A season has about 90 days. This grid gives you 50 days to plan out wellness & grooming things to do to take care of your "ship," your body & soul--whatever you like to call all of it- across a season.

Take care of your Self.
Treat yourself.

Practice Giving a fuck.
For You... LOVE YOU.
First. All else is gravy after you nail that one.

&Log it.

> You'll be fine.
> It is basically
> Doing
> **Something
> Nice to yourself**
> every other
> day. You can
> Handle that

Seasonal Wellness /Self-Care BINGO
[what|when]:

Go.

See.

Do.

Serve.

Travel

Away **Stay-cation** Dream trek

Locale
dates
Transport
Uber budget
[things2 do there]
[things2get b4]

Locale
dates
Transport
Uber budget
[things2 do there]
[things2get b4]

Locale
dates
Transport
Uber budget
[things2 do there]
[things2get b4]

Locale
dates
Transport
Uber budget
[things2 do there]

[things2get b4]

Locale
dates
Transport
Uber budget
[things2 do there]

[things2get b4]

Locale
dates
Transport
Uber budget
[things2 do there]

[things2get b4]

Locale
dates
Transport
Uber budget
[things2 do there]

[things2get b4]

Locale
dates
Transport
Uber budget
[things2 do there]

[things2get b4]

Locale
dates
Transport
Uber budget
[things2 do there]

[things2get b4]

Go.

See.

Do.

Serve.

Travel

Away　　**Stay-cation**　　Dream trek

Locale
dates
Transport
Uber budget
[things2 do there]
[things2get b4]

Locale
dates
Transport
Uber budget
[things2 do there]
[things2get b4]

Locale
dates
Transport
Uber budget
[things2 do there]
[things2get b4]

Locale
dates
Transport
Uber budget
[things2 do there]

[things2get b4]

Locale
dates
Transport
Uber budget
[things2 do there]

[things2get b4]

Locale
dates
Transport
Uber budget
[things2 do there]

[things2get b4]

Locale
dates
Transport
Uber budget
[things2 do there]

[things2get b4]

Locale
dates
Transport
Uber budget
[things2 do there]

[things2get b4]

Locale
dates
Transport
Uber budget
[things2 do there]

[things2get b4]

Seasonal Theme|Ethos:

That ONE big TARGET this season:

Why THIS? Why MUST you hit this?

Break it into 3 parts.

1.   2.   3.

The theme/subject of each part

1.   2.   3.

The ethos [guiding beliefs] of each.

1.   2.   3.

Assign each step to a month & breakdown steps to complete it.

Month			
Theme			
Ethos			
Focus steps 1 2 3 4 5 6			

Seasonal Theme|Ethos:

That ONE big TARGET this season:

Why THIS? Why MUST you hit this?

Break it into 3 parts.

1. 2. 3.

The theme/subject of each part

1. 2. 3.

The ethos [guiding beliefs] of each.

1. 2. 3.

Assign each step to a month & breakdown steps to complete it.

Month			
Theme			
Ethos			
Focus steps			
1			
2			
3			
4			
5			
6			

Seasonal Theme|Ethos:

That ONE big TARGET this season:

Why THIS? Why MUST you hit this?

Break it into 3 parts.

1.   2.   3.

The theme/subject of each part

1.   2.   3.

The ethos[guiding beliefs] of each.

1.   2.   3.

Assign each step to a month & breakdown steps to complete it.

Month			
Theme			
Ethos			
Focus steps			
1			
2			
3			
4			
5			
6			

Seasonal Theme|Ethos:

That ONE big TARGET this season:

Why THIS? Why MUST you hit this?

Break it into 3 parts.

1.   2.   3.

The theme/subject of each part

1.   2.   3.

The ethos [guiding beliefs] of each.

1.   2.   3.

Assign each step to a month & breakdown steps to complete it.

Month			
Theme			
Ethos			
Focus steps 1 2 3 4 5 6			

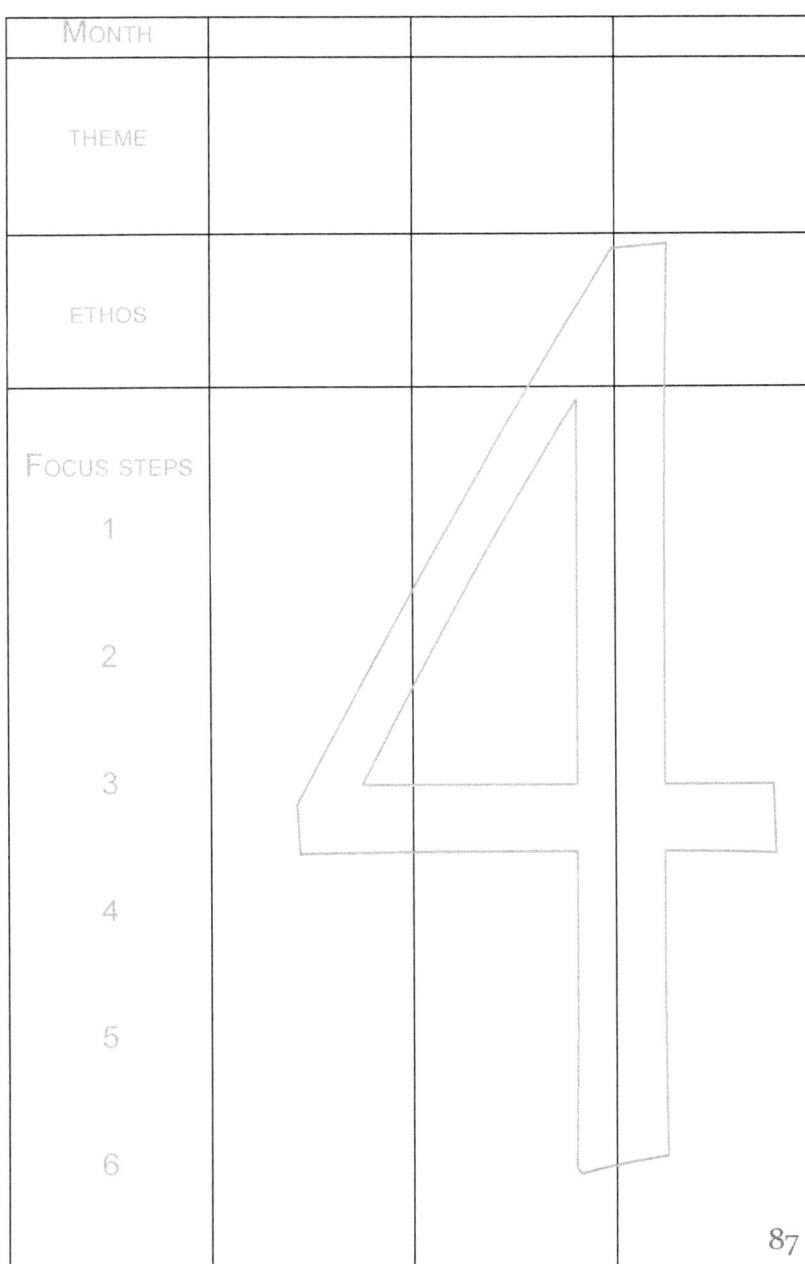

Other "BIGS..."

Big ASK:
Aim to do's

Big TASK:
Gotta do's

Big FLASH:
Show something
Off you're confident
yet shy about.

Big BLAST:
Get to do's

Pick 4 geterdones

Self-care

Sanctuary

Sincere Social Moves

Senseless

Other "BIGS..."

Big ASK:
Aim to do's

Big TASK:
Gotta do's

Big FLASH:
Show something
Off you're confident
yet shy about.

Big BLAST:
Get to do's

Pick 4 geterdones

Self-care | Sanctuary

2

Sincere Social Moves | Senseless

Other "BIGS..."

Big ASK:
Aim to do's

Big TASK:
Gotta do's

Big FLASH:
Show something Off you're confident yet shy about.

Big BLAST:
Get to do's

Pick 4 geterdones

Self-care | Sanctuary

3

Sincere Social Moves | Senseless

Other "BIGS..."

Big ASK:
Aim to do's

Big TASK:
Gotta do's

Big FLASH:
Show something
Off you're confident
yet shy about.

Big BLAST:
Get to do's

Pick 4 geterdones

Self-care

Sanctuary

Sincere Social Moves

Senseless

Project codename:	Magii Specialists **Masterminds** ("Who CAN shoot the dayum dawg?"):	**KNOWN** [Accessible] **INTEL** **Gnosis needed** [people, books, TEDx talks, documentaries, examples]:
	1.	
Dawn: D-Day:	2.	
Modus Operandi [M.O.]:	3.	
	4.	
How2Skin it Steps: E.g., Make a detailed supplies needed list	Dawn/M/D Day 8/22/23/ 9/13 /10/1/23	**New INTEL:** issues & fixes as they arise: e.g., Delivery delays,

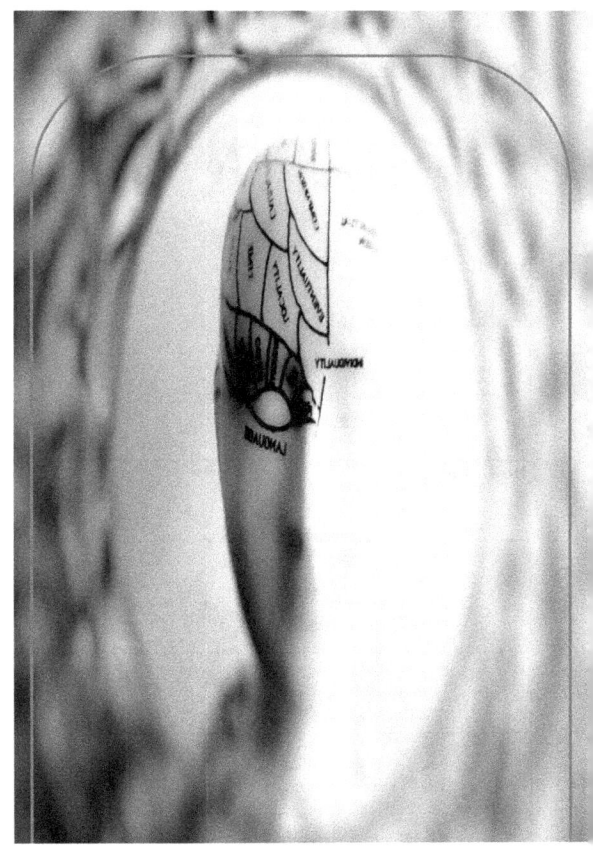

Project codename:	Magii Specialists **Masterminds** ("Who CAN shoot the dayum dawg?"):	**KNOWN** [Accessible] **INTEL** **Gnosis needed** [people, books, TEDx talks, documentaries, examples]:
	1.	
Dawn: D-Day:	2.	
Modus Operandi [M.O.]:	3.	
	4.	
How2Skin it Steps:	Dawn/M/D Day	**New INTEL:** issues & fixes as they arise: e.g., Delivery delays,
E.g., Make a detailed supplies needed list	8/22/23/ 9/13 /10/1/23	

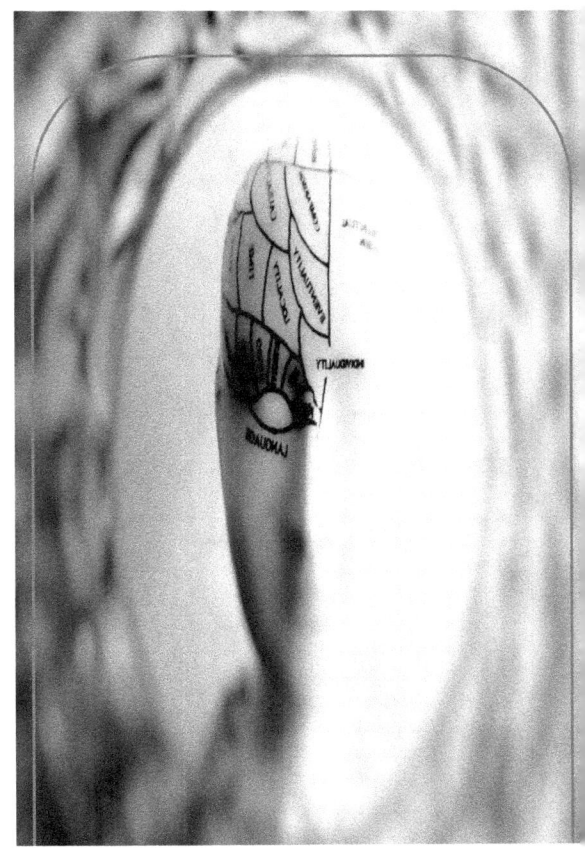

Project codename:	Magii Specialists	KNOWN
	Masterminds ("Who CAN shoot the dayum dawg?"):	[Accessible] **INTEL** **Gnosis needed** [people, books, TEDx talks, documentaries, examples]:
	1.	
Dawn: D-Day:	2.	
Modus Operandi [M.O.]:	3.	
	4.	
How2Skin it Steps: E.g., Make a detailed supplies needed list	**Dawn/M/D Day** 8/22/23/ 9/13 /10/1/23	**New INTEL:** issues & fixes as they arise: e.g., Delivery delays,

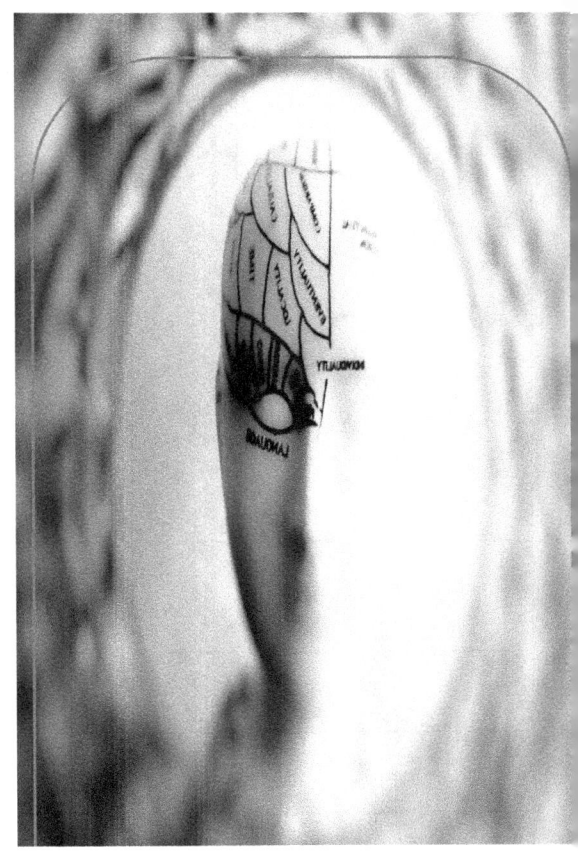

Project codename:	Magii Specialists **Masterminds** ("Who CAN shoot the dayum dawg?"):	**KNOWN** [Accessible] **INTEL** **Gnosis needed** [people, books, TEDx talks, documentaries, examples]:
	1.	
Dawn: D-Day:	2.	
Modus Operandi [M.O.]:	3.	
	4.	
How2Skin it Steps: E.g., Make a detailed supplies needed list	**Dawn/M/D Day** 8/22/23/ 9/13 /10/1/23	**New INTEL:** issues & fixes as they arise: e.g., Delivery delays,

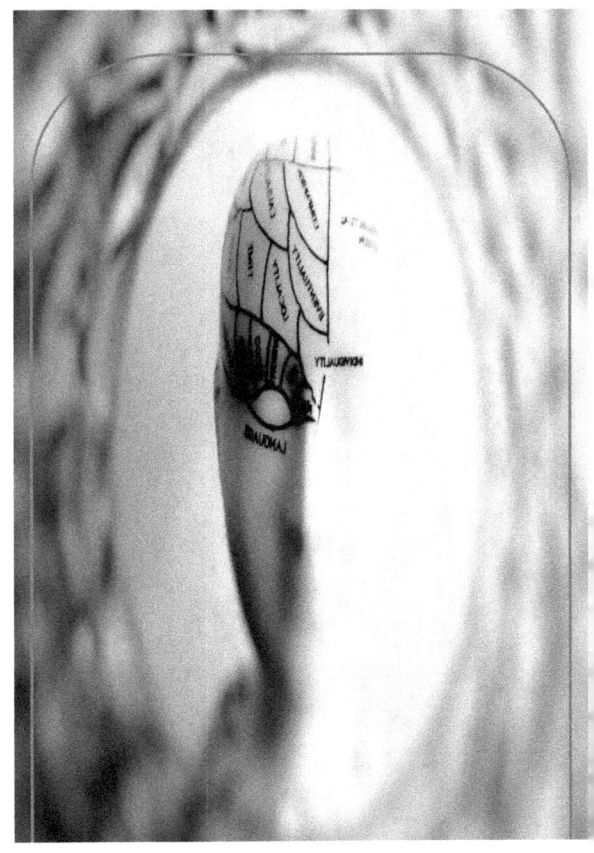

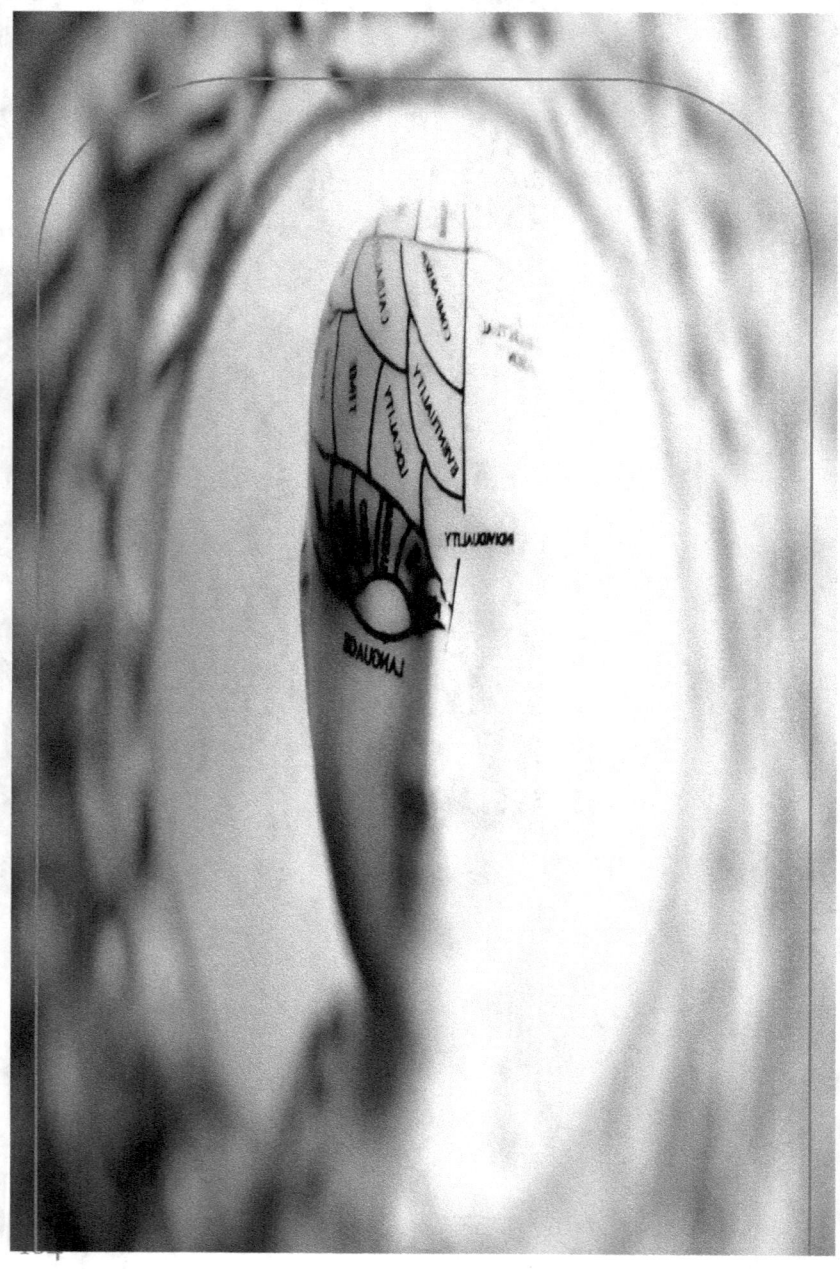

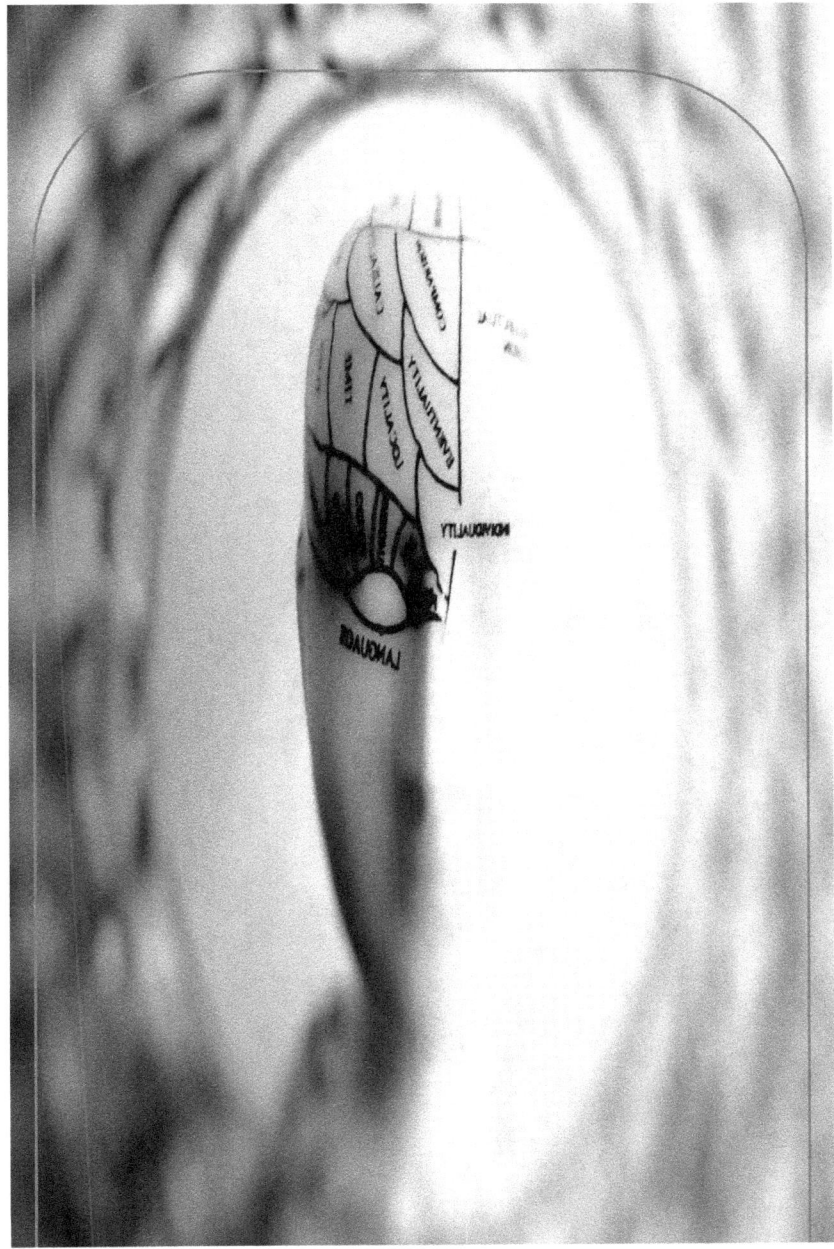

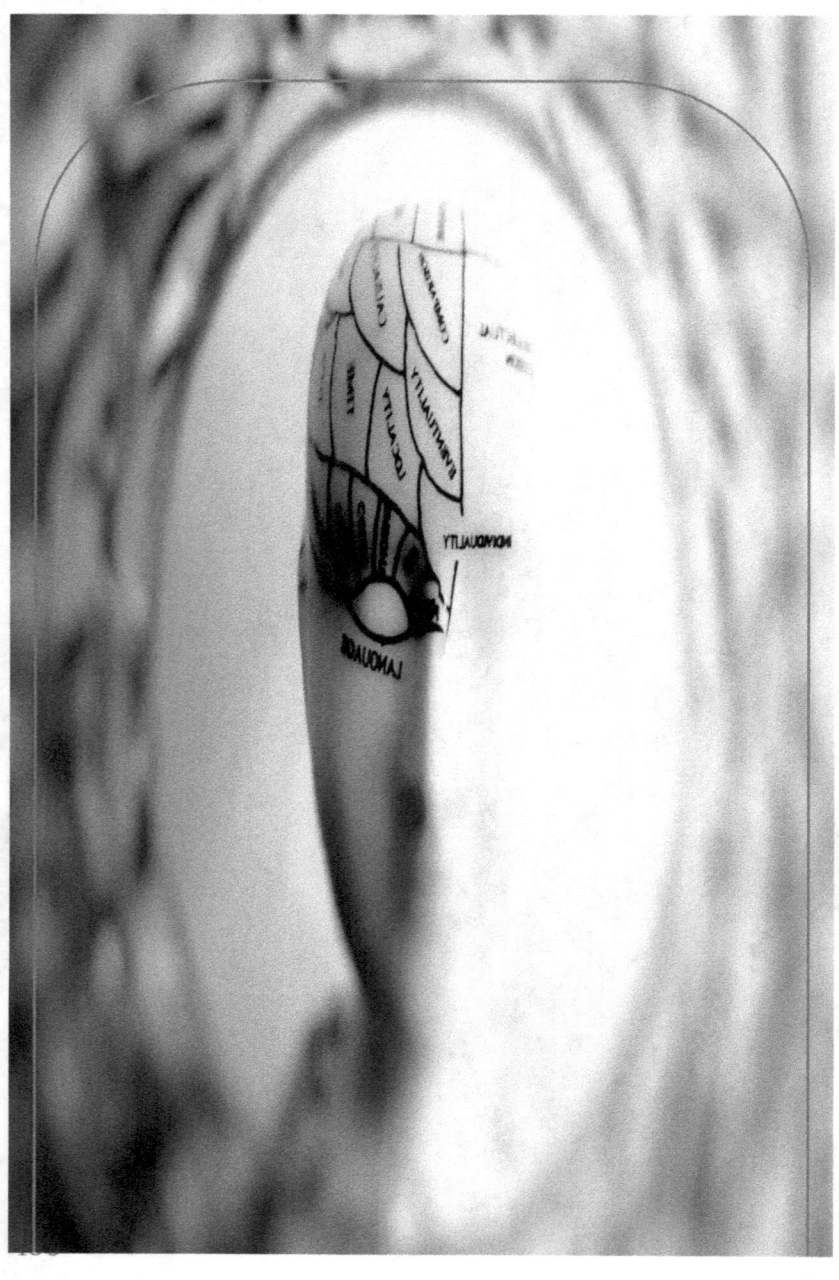

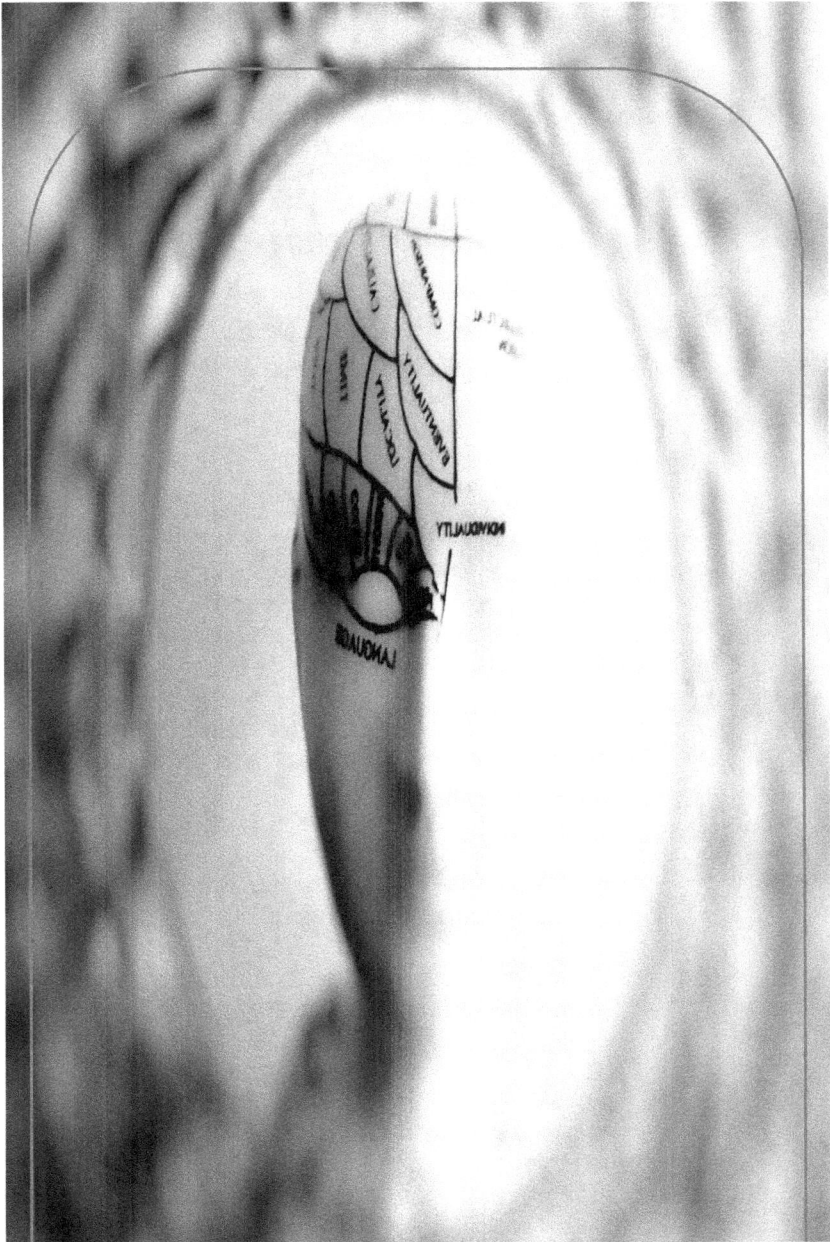

Figure out your FOOD:

ANY directive to sap all the JOY out of food for the sake of "fitting in," or a smaller waistline is utter bullshit.

Yes, Food can be "just fuel" but don't you want to Live a better life than a machine that sits in a garage waiting for oil to be rammed down it's throat so it can run on combustive rage / electrocution through filthy streets it has to drive down?

Yes, I am being a bit ridiculous with the metaphor but the point is...

You deserve more.
You were literally born able to taste everything.
MANY folks temporarily lost the ability to taste (& smell) due to the pandemic but a lot of the habits foisted on us these days falsely labeled as "Healthy" have the same desensitizing effects on us psychologically.

Food is not the enemy, and neither are your taste-buds.
[The food industry? (Kinda, but that's a whole nother can of worms in itself, but...) It doesn't have to be.]

Opting for that better life for you[and yer "machine"] starts with consciously explored better choices made by you down the avenues & aisles you consciously roll.
That's right...quite often you can pick the roads to travel too.
We forget that.

We've all heard it :"Let your food be your medicine~ your medicine be your food!"
Treat this as your **geterdone** deep dive to figure out how to do that~for you.

Ya gotta get some autonomy on this sustenance thing.
...and exercise a little faith.
In yourself, & in literally being given all the things you'd need- In food-
that can help you heal your relationship with it.

Not a doctor. But you're not here to band-aid symptoms. You want to heal the root so your relationship with food can stop being a toxic stumbling block.

Oh. & Do the work... or don't bitch about the absence of glory.
If you are NOT ready to "get this work," respect yourself enough to
Admit that for now and move on. It's totally allowed, & healthier than
A guilt-ridden false start you know you're going to fumble. Move on to something you're less of a punkass about tackling right now, get some success in it and then~ double back to tackle food.

It'll be here, waiting.

Step one: Own what You Like (& loathe)

Maybe you are a true breakfasthead. Maybe the idea of eggs make you want to hurl. Make a list about what you like. Keep it simple & sweet. Pick a meal, a flavor, spice ...something & somewhere to start.

Step two: FIND A COOKBOOK on what you Actually like~

You can buy one [The Globalboho cookbook drops summer 2024(!)], find an old one at a library, even download a cookbook focused on your "thing" for free online. The point is to get a volume of recipes keyed to that thing.

Step three* : 1 PICK a RECIPE! 2 GET the Ingredients! 3 FOLLOW the Instructions! 4 REPEAT!

...yes, I sprung learning to make it on you. If you say you hate cooking, it's the first thing you MUST get over to heal your relationship with food & keep any gains you make re-calibrating your use of food. + Learn to make what you love & you may never go hungry again.

Recipe title/name-

Ingredients

Instructions

Step four: Work through the cookbook

This is a build-able skill. extra worksheets, food logs & shopping lists included.

1x 2x 3x 4x 5x (cross off each time)

Step one: Own what You Like (& loathe)

Maybe you are a true breakfasthead. Maybe the idea of eggs make you want to hurl. Make a list about what you like. Keep it simple & sweet. Pick a meal, a flavor, spice ...something & somewhere to start.

LOG   that   list   here~

Step two: FIND A COOKBOOK on what you Actually like~

List contender cookbooks here~

You can buy one [The Globalboho cookbook drops summer 2024(!)], find an old one at a library, even download a cookbook focused on your "thing" for free online. The point is to get a volume of recipes keyed to that thing.

Step three* : 1 PICK a RECIPE! 2 GET the Ingredients! 3 FOLLOW the Instructions! 4 REPEAT!

...yes, I sprung learning to make it on you. If you say you hate cooking, it's the first thing you MUST get over to heal your relationship with food & keep any gains you make recalibrating your use of food. + Learn to make what you love & you may never go hungry again.

Recipe title/name-

Ingredients

Instructions

Step four: Work through the cookbook

This is a build-able skill. extra worksheets, food logs & shopping lists included.

1x 2x 3x 4x 5x (cross off each time)
110

Step one: Own what You Like (& loathe)

Maybe you are a true breakfasthead. Maybe the idea of eggs make you want to hurl. Make a list about what you like. Keep it simple & sweet. Pick a meal, a flavor, spice ...something & somewhere to start.

Step two: FIND A COOKBOOK on what you Actually like~

You can buy one [The Globalboho cookbook drops summer 2024(!)], find an old one at a library, even download a cookbook focused on your "thing" for free online. The point is to get a volume of recipes keyed to that thing.

Step three*: 1 PICK a RECIPE! 2 GET the Ingredients! 3 FOLLOW the Instructions! 4 REPEAT!

...yes, I sprung learning to make it on you. If you say you hate cooking, it's the first thing you MUST get over to heal your relationship with food & keep any gains you make re-calibrating your use of food.
+ Learn to make what you love & you may never go hungry again.

Recipe title/name-

Ingredients

Instructions

Step four: Work through the cookbook

This is a build-able skill. extra worksheets, food logs & shopping lists included!

1x 2x 3x 4x 5x (cross off each time)

111

Step one: Own what You Like (& loathe)

Maybe you are a true breakfasthead. Maybe the idea of eggs make you want to hurl. Make a list about what you like. Keep it simple & sweet. Pick a meal, a flavor, spice ...something & somewhere to start.

LOG... That list here~

Step two: FIND A COOKBOOK on what you Actually like~

List 3 contender cookbooks here-

You can buy one [The Globalboho cookbook drops summer 2024(!)], find an old one at a library, even download a cookbook focused on your "thing" for free online. The point is to get a volume of recipes keyed to that thing.

Step three* : 1 PICK a RECIPE! 2 GET the Ingredients! 3 FOLLOW the Instructions! 4 REPEAT!

...yes, I sprung learning to make it on you. If you say you hate cooking, it's the first thing you MUST get over to heal your relationship with food & keep any gains you make re-calibrating your use of food. + Learn to make what you love & you may never go hungry again.

Recipe title/name-

Ingredients

Instructions

Step four: Work through the cookbook

This is a build-able skill. extra worksheets, food logs & shopping lists included.

1x 2x 3x 4x 5x (cross off each time)

1st quarter

Free Write

2nd quarter

Free Write

3rd quarter

Free Write

4th quarter

Additional image credit: freepik.

| Free Write

Monthly modus operandi

This month's HIGHEST TIMELINE log line:

Your Life's movie title:

Theme **Year** **Month**

POINT OF THE MONTH:

[NECESSARY] COUNTERPOINT OF THE MONTH:

(EVERY POINT HAS A COUNTERPOINT)

AUDIO BOOK

HAPTIC BOOK

EBOOK:

PODCAST

MOVIE

ODD INTEREST

SPIRITUAL SUBJECT

HERB | FLOWER

CRYSTAL | INCENSE

QUOTE | POET

M	T

Give yourself ONE day a week. Purely For YOU.. One way or another. Find a way.

Harvest Fall Winter Spring Summer **MAR APR MAY**
JUN JUL AUG
I & I DAY
I & I HOUR: FULL MOON **SEP OCT NOV**
HOLY DAYS NEW MOON
BIRTHDAYS etc.,. CYCLE START **DEC JAN FEB**
CYCLE END

W	T	F	S	S
			**Ordered		Due**	

HO ARE YOU?   HOW are YOU EXPRESSING IT?

Revisit, revise, release, readjust, recalibrate…

Last quarter

Free Write

Themes:

Video deep dive teachers:

Full Moon

Date:

- 1. Cleanse your space [Mental & physical].
- 2. Crystals? Charge 'em!.
- 3. Celebrate any wins.
- 4. Release what no longer Serves you.
- 5. Get out in some moonlight.

Free Write

Themes:

Video deep dive teachers:

1st quarter

Themes:

Deep Dive Teachers:

Accepting abundance | Free Write

Free Write

<u>Themes:</u>

<u>Deep Dive Teachers:</u>

New Moon

Date:

1. Imagine what you aim to Bring into your zone..
2. Set new intentions.
3. Journal & Meditate.
4. Scrub &/or soak your body.
5. Get out in some moonlight.

THE MONTH of 12:

NOTES:

"MY BODY CAN"

(OF THE MONTH)

SIFU. SHIFU. COACH. SPIRIT ANIMAL
...
Who is working out with you in your mind's eye? Who's your body inspiration?

THE vibe AIMED 4:

THE PLAYLIST:
1.
2.
3.
4.

Monthly workout mantra:

SUPPLEMENTS Focus:

Workout Focus:
physical therapy
fascia
somatic therapy
lymphatic
massage
rest
stabilization
strength
swimming
walking
running
endurance
dance
cardio
plyometrics
HIIT
cardio
agility
stretching
qigong
yoga
pilates

Monthly workout LOG:

MON	TUE	WED	THU	FRI	SAT	SUN	FOCUS

...the **REST RIT**[UAL]**S**:

"At least ONCE a MONTH I..."

pre | post workout drink LOG

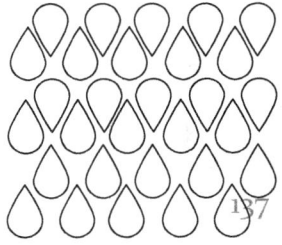

Pick 4 Forms or styles to focus on Getting better with:

E.g.:

Yoga?

Qi Gong?

Stretching?

Swimming?

How many times a week?

How Long?

AM / PM
Intention:

Thought Prompt :

Journal Prompt

Safe word

Synchronicity you'd like to see

Miracles to be on the lookout for

Prayer Requests

sunrise dayUP Geterdone:

Sunset slow down b4BED Geterdone:

Go FI D &/or DO SOMETHING BEAUTIFUL

Curious about it? <u>Learn it</u>

Wish you were able 2 do it? <u>Try it</u>

Place you want 2go? <u>Go 2it</u>

Love to have it outside?<u>Try it @home</u>

Habit 2 improve

Habit 2 give up

Replace with what?

How ?

Accountability:

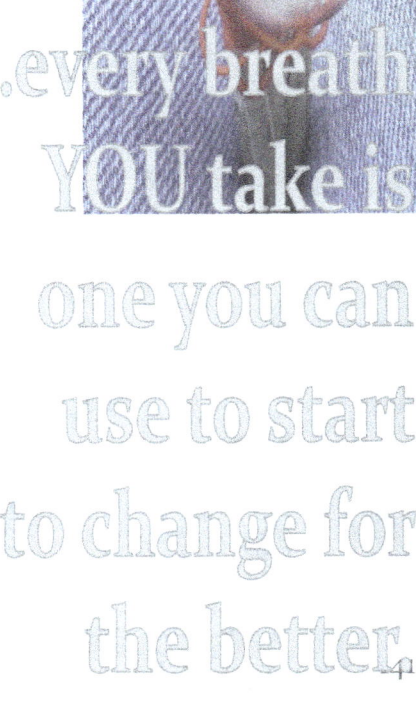

…every breath YOU take is one you can use to start to change for the better.

Theme

Year

Month

This month's HIGHEST TIMELINE log line:

Your Life's movie title:

POINT OF THE MONTH:

[NECESSARY] COUNTERPOINT OF THE MONTH:

(EVERY POINT HAS A COUNTERPOINT)

- AUDIO BOOK
- HAPTIC BOOK
- EBOOK:
- PODCAST
- MOVIE
- ODD INTEREST
- SPIRITUAL SUBJECT
- HERB | FLOWER
- CRYSTAL | INCENSE
- QUOTE | POET

M	T

Give yourself ONE day a week. Purely For YOU.. One way or another. Find a way.

Harvest Fall Winter Spring Summer

MAR APR MAY
JUN JUL AUG
SEP OCT NOV
DEC JAN FEB

I & I DAY
I & I HOUR:
HOLY DAYS
BIRTHDAYS etc.,.

FULL MOON
NEW MOON
CYCLE START
CYCLE END

W	T	F	S	S
			Ordered || Due	

WHO ARE YOU?   HOW are YOU EXPRESSING IT?

Revisit, revise, release, re-adjust, re-calibrate...

Last quarter

Free Write

Themes:

Video deep dive teachers:

Full Moon

Date:

1. Cleanse your space [Mental & physical].

2. Crystals? Charge 'em!.

3. Celebrate any wins.

4. Release what no longer Serves you.

5. Get out in some moonlight.

Free Write

Themes:

Video deep dive teachers:

1st quarter

Themes:

Deep Dive Teachers:

Accepting abundance | Free Write

Free Write

<u>Themes:</u>

<u>Deep Dive Teachers:</u>

THE MONTH of 12:

NOTES:

"MY BODY CAN"

(OF THE MONTH)

SIFU. SHIFU. COACH. SPIRIT ANIMAL
...
Who is working out with you in your mind's eye? Who's your body inspiration?

THE vibe AIMED 4:

THE PLAYLIST:
1.
2.
3.
4.

Monthly workout mantra:

SUPPLEMENTS Focus:

Workout Focus:
physical therapy
fascia
somatic therapy
lymphatic
massage
rest
stabilization
strength
swimming
walking
running
endurance
dance
cardio
plyometrics
HIIT
cardio
agility
stretching
qigong
yoga
pilates

Monthly workout LOG:

MON	TUE	WED	THU	FRI	SAT	SUN	FOCUS

...the **REST RIT**[UAL]**S**:

"At least ONCE a MONTH I..."

pre | post workout drink LOG

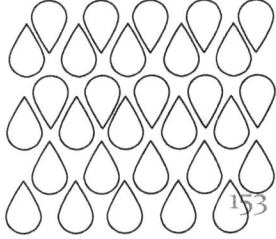

Pick 4 Forms or styles to focus on Getting better with:

E.g.:

Yoga?

Qi Gong?

Stretching?

Swimming?

How many times a week?

How Long?

AM / PM
Intention:

Thought Prompt :

Journal Prompt

Safe word

Synchronicity you'd like to see

Miracles to be on the lookout for

Prayer Requests

sunrise dayUP Geterdone:

Sunset slow down b4BED Geterdone:

Go FI D &/or DO SOMETHING BEAUTIFUL

Curious about it? <u>Learn it</u>

Wish you were able 2 do it? <u>Try it</u>

Place you want 2go? <u>Go 2it</u>

Love to have it outside? <u>Try it @home</u>

Habit 2 improve

Habit 2 give up

Replace with what?

How ?

Accountability:

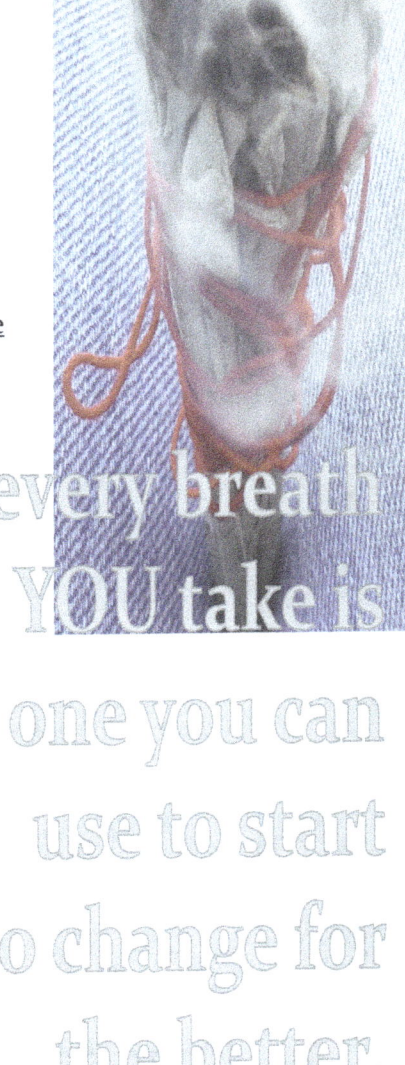

...every breath YOU take is one you can use to start to change for the better.

Theme   Year   Month

POINT OF THE MONTH:

[NECESSARY] COUNTERPOINT OF THE MONTH:

(EVERY POINT HAS A COUNTERPOINT)

AUDIO BOOK

HAPTIC BOOK

EBOOK:

PODCAST

MOVIE

ODD INTEREST

SPIRITUAL SUBJECT

HERB | FLOWER

CRYSTAL | INCENSE

QUOTE | POET

This month's HIGHEST TIMELINE log line:

Your Life's movie title:

M	T

Give yourself ONE day a week. Purely For YOU.. One way or another. Find a way.

Harvest Fall Winter Spring Summer

**MAR APR MAY
JUN JUL AUG
SEP OCT NOV
DEC JAN FEB**

I & I DAY
I & I HOUR:
HOLY DAYS
BIRTHDAYS etc.,.

FULL MOON
NEW MOON
CYCLE START
CYCLE END

W	T	F	S	S
			**Ordered		Due**	

HO ARE YOU?   **HOW are YOU EXPRESSING IT?**

Revisit, revise, release, re-adjust, recalibrate...

Last quarter

Free Write

Themes:

Video deep dive teachers:

Full Moon

Date:

1. Cleanse your space [Mental & physical].

2. Crystals? Charge 'em!.

3. Celebrate any wins.

4. Release what no longer Serves you.

5. Get out in some moonlight.

Free Write

Themes:

Video deep dive teachers:

1st quarter

Themes:

Deep Dive Teachers:

Accepting abundance | Free Write

Free Write

<u>Themes:</u>

<u>Deep Dive Teachers:</u>

THE MONTH of 12:
"MY BODY CAN"

NOTES:

(OF THE MONTH)

SIFU. SHIFU. COACH. SPIRIT ANIMAL
...
Who is working out with you in your mind's eye? Who's your body inspiration?

THE vibe AIMED 4:

THE PLAYLIST:
1.
2.
3.
4.

Monthy workout mantra:

SUPPLEMENTS Focus:

Workout Focus:
physical therapy
fascia
somatic therapy
lymphatic
massage
rest
stabilization
strength
swimming
walking
running
endurance
dance
cardio
plyometrics
HIIT
cardio
agility
stretching
qigong
yoga
pilates

MON	TUE	WED	THU	FRI	SAT	SUN	FOCUS

Monthly workout LOG:

...the REST RIT[UAL]S:

"At least ONCE a MONTH I..."

pre | post workout drink LOG

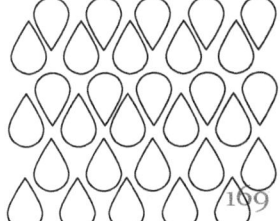

Pick 4 Forms or styles to focus on Getting better with:

E.g.:

Yoga?

Qi Gong?

Stretching?

Swimming?

How many times a week?

How Long?

AM / PM
Intention:

Thought Prompt :

Journal Prompt

Safe word

Synchronicity you'd like to see

Miracles to be on the lookout for

Prayer Requests

sunrise dayUP Geterdone:

Sunset slow down b4BED Geterdone:

Go FI D &/or DO SOMETHING BEAUTIFUL

Curious about it? <u>Learn it</u>

Wish you were able 2 do it? <u>Try it</u>

Place you want 2go? <u>Go 2it</u>

Love to have it outside? <u>Try it @home</u>

Habit 2 improve

Habit 2 give up

Replace with what?

How ?

Accountability:

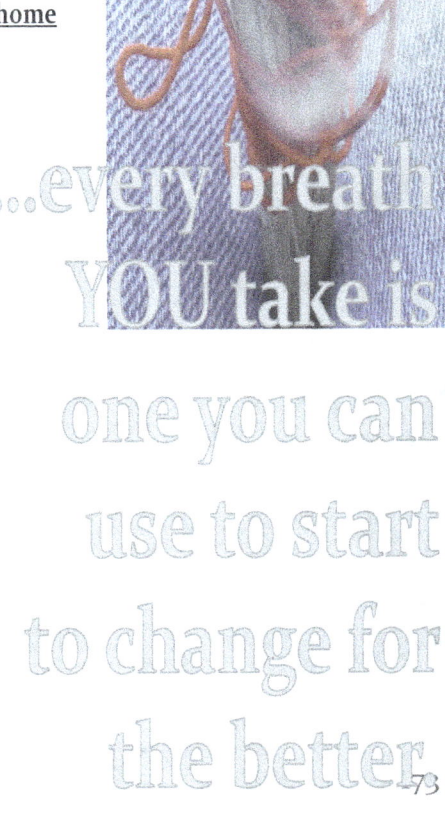

...every breath YOU take is one you can use to start to change for the better.

Theme   Year   Month

POINT OF THE MONTH:

[NECESSARY] COUNTERPOINT OF THE MONTH:

(EVERY POINT HAS A COUNTERPOINT)

AUDIO BOOK

HAPTIC BOOK

EBOOK:

PODCAST

MOVIE

ODD INTEREST

SPIRITUAL SUBJECT

HERB | FLOWER

CRYSTAL | INCENSE

QUOTE | POET

This month's HIGHEST TIMELINE log line:

Your Life's movie title:

M	T

Give yourself ONE day a week. Purely For YOU.. One way or another. Find a way.

Harvest Fall Winter Spring Summer

MAR APR MAY
JUN JUL AUG
SEP OCT NOV
DEC JAN FEB

I & I DAY
I & I HOUR:
HOLY DAYS
BIRTHDAYS etc.,.

FULL MOON
NEW MOON
CYCLE START
CYCLE END

W	T	F	S	S
			Ordered || Due	

HO ARE YOU?   HOW are YOU EXPRESSING IT?

Free Write

Themes:

Video deep dive teachers:

Full Moon

Date:

1. Cleanse your space [Mental & physical].

2. Crystals? Charge 'em!.

3. Celebrate any wins.

4. Release what no longer Serves you.

5. Get out in some moonlight.

Free Write

Themes:

Video deep dive teachers:

1st quarter

Themes:

Deep Dive Teachers:

Accepting abundance | Free Write

Free Write

Themes:

Deep Dive Teachers:

New Moon

Date:

1. Imagine what you aim to Bring into your zone..
2. Set new intentions.
3. Journal & Meditate.
4. Scrub &/or soak your body.
5. Get out in some moonlight.

THE MONTH of 12:

NOTES:

"MY BODY CAN"

(OF THE MONTH)

SIFU. SHIFU. COACH. SPIRIT ANIMAL
...
Who is working out with you in your mind's eye? Who's your body inspiration?

THE vibe AIMED 4:

THE PLAYLIST:
1.
2.
3.
4.

Monthly workout mantra:

SUPPLEMENTS Focus:

Workout Focus:
physical therapy
fascia
somatic therapy
lymphatic
massage
rest
stabilization
strength
swimming
walking
running
endurance
dance
cardio
plyometrics
HIIT
cardio
agility
stretching
qigong
yoga
pilates

Monthly workout LOG

MON	TUE	WED	THU	FRI	SAT	SUN	FOCUS

...the REST RIT[UAL]S:

"At least ONCE a MONTH I..."

pre | post workout drink LOG

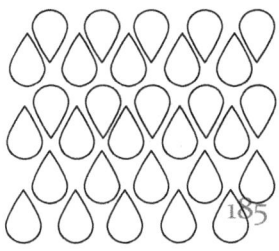

Pick 4 Forms or styles to focus on Getting better with:

E.g.:

Yoga?

Qi Gong?

Stretching?

Swimming?

How many times a week?

How Long?

AM / PM
Intention:

Thought Prompt :

Journal Prompt

Safe word

Synchronicity you'd like to see

Miracles to be on the lookout for

Prayer Requests

sunrise dayUP Geterdone:

Sunset slow down b4BED Geterdone:

Go FI D &/or DO SOMETHING BEAUTIFUL

Curious about it? <u>Learn it</u>

Wish you were able 2 do it? <u>Try it</u>

Place you want 2go? <u>Go 2it</u>

Love to have it outside?<u>Try it @home</u>

Habit 2 improve

Habit 2 give up

Replace with what?

How ?

Accountability:

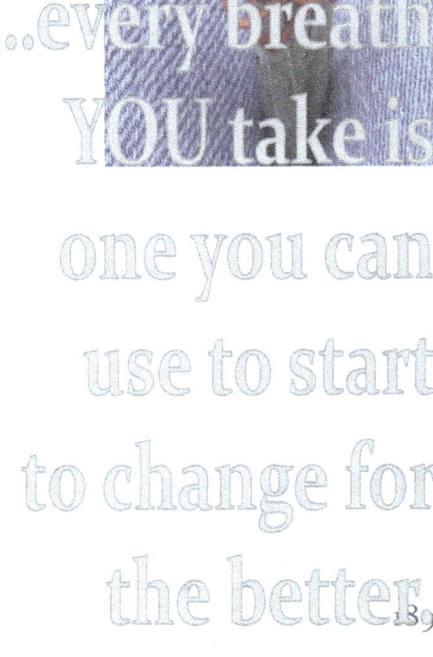

...every breath YOU take is one you can use to start to change for the better.

Theme **Year** **Month**

This month's HIGHEST TIMELINE log line:

Your Life's movie title:

POINT OF THE MONTH:

[NECESSARY] COUNTERPOINT OF THE MONTH:

(EVERY POINT HAS A COUNTERPOINT)

AUDIO BOOK

HAPTIC BOOK

EBOOK:

PODCAST

MOVIE

ODD INTEREST

SPIRITUAL SUBJECT

HERB | FLOWER

CRYSTAL | INCENSE

QUOTE | POET

M	T

Give yourself ONE day a week. Purely For YOU.. One way or another. Find a way.

Harvest Fall Winter Spring Summer

MAR APR MAY
JUN JUL AUG
SEP OCT NOV
DEC JAN FEB

I & I DAY
I & I HOUR:
HOLY DAYS
BIRTHDAYS etc.,.

FULL MOON
NEW MOON
CYCLE START
CYCLE END

W	T	F	S	S
			Ordered | | Due	

'HO ARE YOU?   HOW are YOU EXPRESSING IT?

Revisit, revise, release, re-adjust, re-calibrate…

Last quarter

Free Write

Themes:

Video deep dive teachers:

Full Moon

Date:

1. Cleanse your space [Mental & physical].

2. Crystals? Charge 'em!.

3. Celebrate any wins.

4. Release what no longer Serves you.

5. Get out in some moonlight.

Free Write

Themes:

Video deep dive teachers:

1st quarter

Themes:

Deep Dive Teachers:

Free Write

Themes:

Deep Dive Teachers:

THE MONTH of 12:

"MY BODY CAN"

(OF THE MONTH)

NOTES:

SIFU. SHIFU. COACH. SPIRIT ANIMAL
...
Who is working out with you in your mind's eye? Who's your body inspiration?

THE vibe AIMED 4:

THE PLAYLIST:
1.
2.
3.
4.

Monthy workout mantra:

SUPPLEMENTS Focus:

Workout Focus:
physical therapy
fascia
somatic therapy
lymphatic
massage
rest
stabilization
strength
swimming
walking
running
endurance
dance
cardio
plyometrics
HIIT
cardio
agility
stretching
qigong
yoga
pilates

Monthly workout LOG:

MON	TUE	WED	THU	FRI	SAT	SUN	FOCUS

...the **REST RIT**[UAL]**S**:

"At least ONCE a MONTH I..."

pre | post workout drink LOG

201

Pick 4 Forms or styles to focus on Getting better with:

E.g.:

Yoga?

Qi Gong?

Stretching?

Swimming?

How many times a week?

How Long?

AM / PM
Intention:

Thought Prompt :

Journal Prompt

Safe word

Synchronicity you'd like to see

Miracles to be on the lookout for

Prayer Requests

sunrise dayUP Geterdone:

Sunset slow down b4BED Geterdone:

Go FIND &/or DO SOMETHING BEAUTIFUL

Curious about it? <u>Learn it</u>

Wish you were able 2 do it? <u>Try it</u>

Place you want 2go? <u>Go 2it</u>

Love to have it outside?<u>Try it @home</u>

Habit 2 improve

Habit 2 give up

Replace with what?

How ?

Accountability:

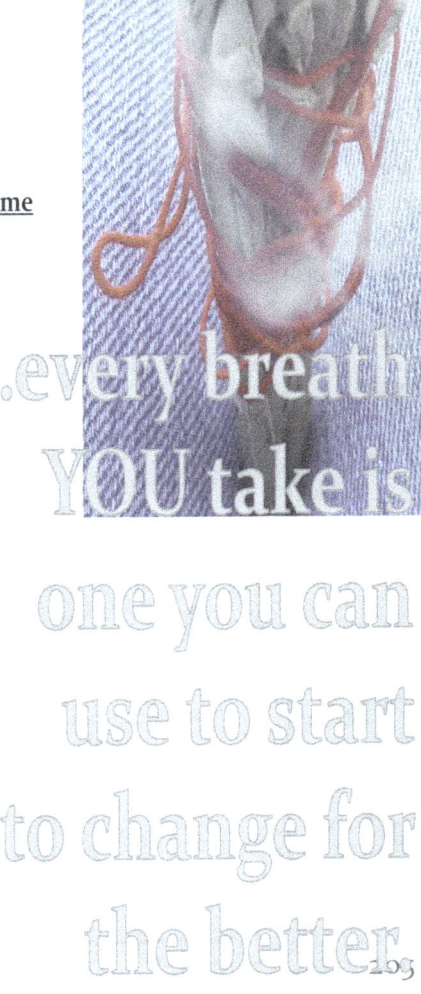

…every breath YOU take is one you can use to start to change for the better.

Theme

Year

Month

POINT OF THE MONTH:

[NECESSARY] COUNTERPOINT OF THE MONTH:

(EVERY POINT HAS A COUNTERPOINT)

AUDIO BOOK

HAPTIC BOOK

EBOOK:

PODCAST

MOVIE

ODD INTEREST

SPIRITUAL SUBJECT

HERB | FLOWER

CRYSTAL | INCENSE

QUOTE | POET

This month's HIGHEST TIMELINE log line:

Your Life's movie title:

M	T

Give yourself ONE day a week. Purely For YOU.. One way or another. Find a way.

Harvest Fall Winter Spring Summer

MAR APR MAY
JUN JUL AUG
SEP OCT NOV
DEC JAN FEB

I & I DAY
I & I HOUR:
HOLY DAYS
BIRTHDAYS etc.,.

FULL MOON
NEW MOON
CYCLE START
CYCLE END

W	T	F	S	S
			Ordered | | Due	

HO ARE YOU?   **HOW are YOU EXPRESSING IT?**

Revisit, revise, release, re-adjust, re-calibrate...

Last quarter

Free Write

Themes:

Video deep dive teachers:

Full Moon

Date:

1. Cleanse your space [Mental & physical].

2. Crystals? Charge 'em!.

3. Celebrate any wins.

4. Release what no longer Serves you.

5. Get out in some moonlight.

Free Write

Themes:

Video deep dive teachers:

1st quarter

Themes:

Deep Dive Teachers:

Free Write

<u>Themes:</u>

<u>Deep Dive Teachers:</u>

New Moon

Date:

1. Imagine what you aim to Bring into your zone..
2. Set new intentions.
3. Journal & Meditate.
4. Scrub &/or soak your body.
5. Get out in some moonlight.

THE MONTH of 12:
"MY BODY CAN"
(OF THE MONTH)

NOTES:

SIFU. SHIFU. COACH. SPIRIT ANIMAL
...
Who is working out with you in your mind's eye? Who's your body inspiration?

THE vibe AIMED 4:

THE PLAYLIST:
1.
2.
3.
4.

Monthy workout mantra:

SUPPLEMENTS Focus:

Workout Focus:
physical therapy
fascia
somatic therapy
lymphatic
massage
rest
stabilization
strength
swimming
walking
running
endurance
dance
cardio
plyometrics
HIIT
cardio
agility
stretching
qigong
yoga
pilates

MON	TUE	WED	THU	FRI	SAT	SUN	FOCUS

Monthly workout LOG:

...the REST RIT[UAL]S:

"At least ONCE a MONTH I..."

pre | post workout drink LOG

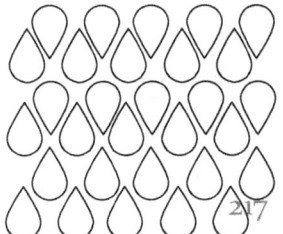

Pick 4 Forms or styles to focus on Getting better with:

E.g.:

Yoga?

Qi Gong?

Stretching?

Swimming?

How many times a week?

How Long?

AM / PM
Intention:

Thought Prompt :

Journal Prompt

Safe word

Synchronicity you'd like to see

Miracles to be on the lookout for

Prayer Requests

sunrise dayUP Geterdone:

Sunset slow down b4BED Geterdone:

Go FI D &/or DO SOMETHING BEAUTIFUL

Curious about it? <u>Learn it</u>

Wish you were able 2 do it? <u>Try it</u>

Place you want 2go? <u>Go 2it</u>

Love to have it outside? <u>Try it @home</u>

Habit 2 improve

Habit 2 give up

Replace with what?

How ?

Accountability:

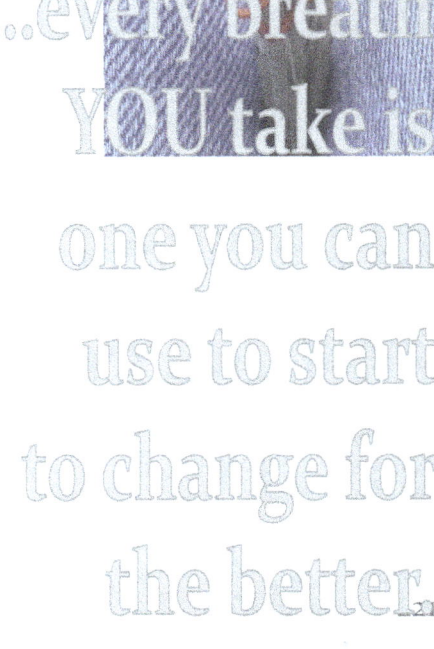

...every breath YOU take is one you can use to start to change for the better.

Theme

Year

Month

POINT OF THE MONTH:

[NECESSARY] COUNTERPOINT OF THE MONTH:

(EVERY POINT HAS A COUNTERPOINT)

AUDIO BOOK

HAPTIC BOOK

EBOOK:

PODCAST

MOVIE

ODD INTEREST

SPIRITUAL SUBJECT

HERB | FLOWER

CRYSTAL | INCENSE

QUOTE | POET

This month's HIGHEST TIMELINE log line:

Your Life's movie title:

M	T

Give yourself ONE day a week. Purely For YOU.. One way or another. Find a way.

Harvest Fall Winter Spring Summer

MAR APR MAY
JUN JUL AUG
SEP OCT NOV
DEC JAN FEB

I & I DAY
I & I HOUR:
HOLY DAYS
BIRTHDAYS etc.,.

FULL MOON
NEW MOON
CYCLE START
CYCLE END

W	T	F	S	S
			Ordered || Due	

HO ARE YOU?   HOW are YOU EXPRESSING IT?

Revisit, revise, release, readjust, recalibrate...

Last quarter

Free Write

Themes:

Video deep dive teachers:

Full Moon

Date:

- 1. Cleanse your space [Mental & physical].
- 2. Crystals? Charge 'em!.
- 3. Celebrate any wins.
- 4. Release what no longer Serves you.
- 5. Get out in some moonlight.

Free Write

Themes:

Video deep dive teachers:

1st quarter

Themes:

Deep Dive Teachers:

Accepting abundance | Free Write

Free Write

Themes:

Deep Dive Teachers:

THE MONTH of 12:

NOTES:

(OF THE MONTH)

SIFU. SHIFU. COACH. SPIRIT ANIMAL
...
Who is working out with you in your mind's eye? Who's your body inspiration?

THE vibe AIMED 4:

THE PLAYLIST:
1.
2.
3.
4.

Monthly workout mantra:

SUPPLEMENTS Focus:

Workout Focus:
physical therapy
fascia
somatic therapy
lymphatic
massage
rest
stabilization
strength
swimming
walking
running
endurance
dance
cardio
plyometrics
HIIT
cardio
agility
stretching
qigong
yoga
pilates

Monthly workout LOG:

MON	TUE	WED	THU	FRI	SAT	SUN	FOCUS

...the REST RIT[UAL]S:

"At least ONCE a MONTH I..."

pre | post workout drink LOG

Pick 4 Forms or styles to focus on Getting better with:

E.g.:

Yoga?

Qi Gong?

Stretching?

Swimming?

How many times a week?

How Long?

AM / PM
Intention:

Thought Prompt :

Journal Prompt

Safe word

Synchronicity you'd like to see

Miracles to be on the lookout for

Prayer Requests

sunrise dayUP Geterdone:

Sunset slow down b4BED Geterdone:

Go FI D &/or DO SOMETHING BEAUTIFUL

Curious about it? <u>Learn it</u>

Wish you were able 2 do it? <u>Try it</u>

Place you want 2go? <u>Go 2it</u>

Love to have it outside?<u>Try it @home</u>

Habit 2 improve

Habit 2 give up

Replace with what?

How ?

Accountability:

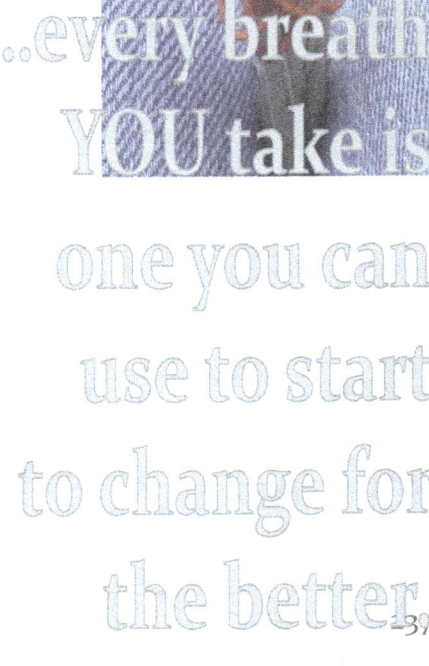

...every breath YOU take is one you can use to start to change for the better.

Theme

Year

Month

POINT OF THE MONTH:

[NECESSARY] COUNTERPOINT OF THE MONTH:

(EVERY POINT HAS A COUNTERPOINT)

AUDIO BOOK

HAPTIC BOOK

EBOOK:

PODCAST

MOVIE

ODD INTEREST

SPIRITUAL SUBJECT

HERB | FLOWER

CRYSTAL | INCENSE

QUOTE | POET

This month's HIGHEST TIMELINE log line:

Your Life's movie title:

M	T

Give yourself ONE day a week. Purely For YOU.. One way or another. Find a way.

Harvest Fall Winter Spring Summer

**MAR APR MAY
JUN JUL AUG
SEP OCT NOV
DEC JAN FEB**

I & I DAY
I & I HOUR:
HOLY DAYS
BIRTHDAYS etc.,.

FULL MOON
NEW MOON
CYCLE START
CYCLE END

W	T	F	S	S
			Ordered ||Due	

WHO ARE YOU?   HOW are YOU EXPRESSING IT?

Revisit, revise, release, re-adjust, re-calibrate...

Last quarter

Free Write

Themes:

Video deep dive teachers:

Full Moon

Date:

- 1. Cleanse your space [Mental & physical].
- 2. Crystals? Charge 'em!.
- 3. Celebrate any wins.
- 4. Release what no longer Serves you.
- 5. Get out in some moonlight.

Free Write

Themes:

Video deep dive teachers:

1st quarter

Themes:

Deep Dive Teachers:

Accepting abundance | Free Write

Free Write

Themes:

Deep Dive Teachers:

THE MONTH of 12:

"MY BODY CAN"

NOTES:

(OF THE MONTH)

SIFU. SHIFU. COACH. SPIRIT ANIMAL
...
Who is working out with you in your mind's eye? Who's your body inspiration?

THE vibe AIMED 4:

THE PLAYLIST:
1.
2.
3.
4.

Monthly workout mantra:

SUPPLEMENTS Focus:

Workout Focus:
physical therapy
fascia
somatic therapy
lymphatic
massage
rest
stabilization
strength
swimming
walking
running
endurance
dance
cardio
plyometrics
HIIT
cardio
agility
stretching
qigong
yoga
pilates

MON	TUE	WED	THU	FRI	SAT	SUN	FOCUS

...the **REST RIT[UAL]S:**

"At least ONCE a MONTH I..."

pre | post workout drink LOG

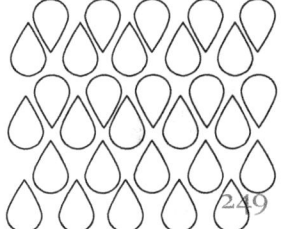

Pick 4 Forms or styles to focus on Getting better with:

E.g.:

Yoga?

Qi Gong?

Stretching?

Swimming?

How many times a week?

How Long?

AM / PM
Intention:

Thought Prompt :

Journal Prompt

Safe word

Synchronicity you'd like to see

Miracles to be on the lookout for

Prayer Requests

<u>sunrise dayUP Geterdone:</u>

<u>Sunset slow down b4BED Geterdone:</u>

Go FI D &/or DO SOMETHING BEAUTIFUL

Curious about it? <u>Learn it</u>

Wish you were able 2 do it? <u>Try it</u>

Place you want 2go? <u>Go 2it</u>

Love to have it outside?<u>Try it @home</u>

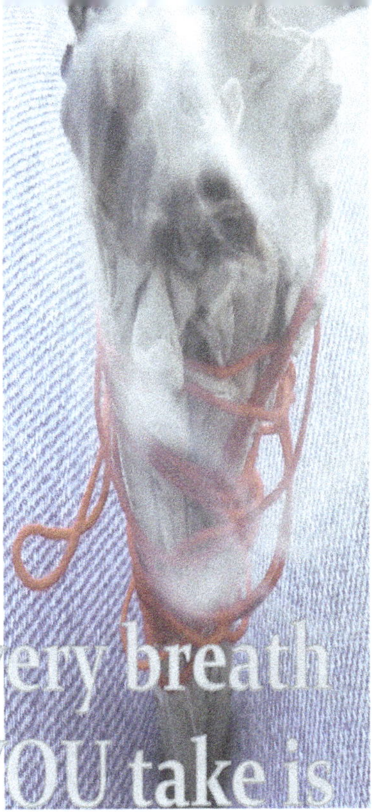

Habit 2 improve

Habit 2 give up

Replace with what?

How ?

Accountability:

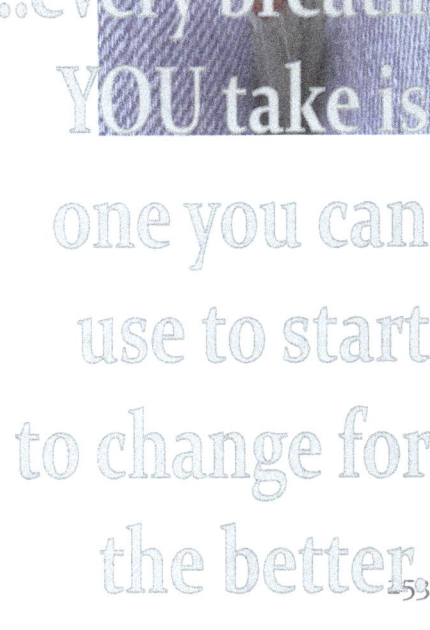

...every breath YOU take is one you can use to start to change for the better

Theme

Year

Month

POINT OF THE MONTH:

[NECESSARY] COUNTERPOINT OF THE MONTH:

(EVERY POINT HAS A COUNTERPOINT)

- AUDIO BOOK
- HAPTIC BOOK
- EBOOK:
- PODCAST
- MOVIE
- ODD INTEREST
- SPIRITUAL SUBJECT
- HERB | FLOWER
- CRYSTAL | INCENSE
- QUOTE | POET

This month's HIGHEST TIMELINE log line:

Your Life's movie title:

M	T

Give yourself ONE day a week. Purely For YOU.. One way or another. Find a way.

Harvest Fall Winter Spring Summer

MAR APR MAY JUN JUL AUG SEP OCT NOV DEC JAN FEB

I & I DAY
I & I HOUR:
HOLY DAYS
BIRTHDAYS etc.,.

FULL MOON
NEW MOON
CYCLE START
CYCLE END

W	T	F	S	S
			**Ordered		Due**	

HO ARE YOU?   **HOW are YOU EXPRESSING IT?**

Revisit, revise, release, re-adjust, re-calibrate...

Last quarter

Free Write

Themes:

Video deep dive teachers:

Full Moon

Date:

- 1. Cleanse your space [Mental & physical].
- 2. Crystals? Charge 'em!.
- 3. Celebrate any wins.
- 4. Release what no longer Serves you.
- 5. Get out in some moonlight.

Free Write

Themes:

Video deep dive teachers:

1st quarter

Themes:

Deep Dive Teachers:

Free Write

Themes:

Deep Dive Teachers:

New Moon

Date:

1. Imagine what you aim to Bring into your zone..

2. Set new intentions.

3. Journal & Meditate.

4. Scrub &/or soak your body.

5. Get out in some moonlight.

THE MONTH of 12:

NOTES:

"MY BODY CAN"

(OF THE MONTH)

SIFU. SHIFU. COACH. SPIRIT ANIMAL
...
Who is working out with you in your mind's eye? Who's your body inspiration?

THE vibe AIMED 4:

THE PLAYLIST:
1.
2.
3.
4.

Monthy workout mantra:

SUPPLEMENTS Focus:

Workout Focus:
physical therapy
fascia
somatic therapy
lymphatic
massage
rest
stabilization
strength
swimming
walking
running
endurance
dance
cardio
plyometrics
HIIT
cardio
agility
stretching
qigong
yoga
pilates

Monthly workout LOG:

MON	TUE	WED	THU	FRI	SAT	SUN	FOCUS

...the REST RIT[UAL]S:

"At least ONCE a MONTH I..."

pre | post workout drink LOG

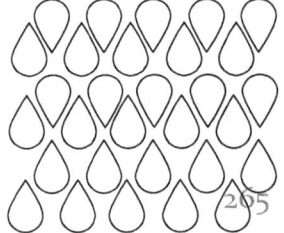

Pick 4 Forms or styles to focus on Getting better with:

E.g.:

Yoga?

Qi Gong?

Stretching?

Swimming?

How many times a week?

How Long?

AM / PM
Intention:

Thought Prompt :

Journal Prompt

Safe word

Synchronicity you'd like to see

Miracles to be on the lookout for

Prayer Requests

sunrise dayUP Geterdone:

Sunset slow down b4BED Geterdone:

Go FI D &/or DO SOMETHING BEAUTIFUL

Curious about it? <u>Learn it</u>

Wish you were able 2 do it? <u>Try it</u>

Place you want 2go? <u>Go 2it</u>

Love to have it outside?<u>Try it @home</u>

Habit 2 improve

Habit 2 give up

Replace with what?

How ?

Accountability:

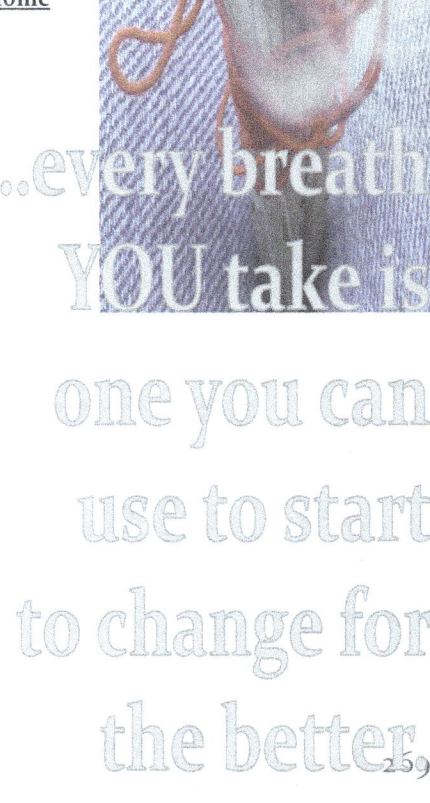

…every breath YOU take is one you can use to start to change for the better.

This month's HIGHEST TIMELINE log line:

Your Life's movie title:

Theme
Year
Month

POINT OF THE MONTH:

[NECESSARY] COUNTERPOINT OF THE MONTH:

(EVERY POINT HAS A COUNTERPOINT)

AUDIO BOOK

HAPTIC BOOK

EBOOK:

PODCAST

MOVIE

ODD INTEREST

SPIRITUAL SUBJECT

HERB | FLOWER

CRYSTAL | INCENSE

QUOTE | POET

M	T

Give yourself ONE day a week. Purely For YOU.. One way or another. Find a way.

Harvest Fall Winter Spring Summer

MAR APR MAY
JUN JUL AUG
SEP OCT NOV
DEC JAN FEB

I & I DAY
I & I HOUR:
HOLY DAYS
BIRTHDAYS etc.,.

FULL MOON
NEW MOON
CYCLE START
CYCLE END

W	T	F	S	S
			Ordered ||Due	

HO ARE YOU?   HOW are YOU EXPRESSING IT?

Revisit, revise, release, readjust, re-calibrate...

Last quarter

Free Write

Themes:

Video deep dive teachers:

Full Moon

Date:

- 1. Cleanse your space [Mental & physical].
- 2. Crystals? Charge 'em!.
- 3. Celebrate any wins.
- 4. Release what no longer Serves you.
- 5. Get out in some moonlight.

Free Write

Themes:

Video deep dive teachers:

1st quarter

Themes:

Deep Dive Teachers:

Free Write

Themes:

Deep Dive Teachers:

THE MONTH of 12:

NOTES:

"MY BODY CAN"

(OF THE MONTH)

SIFU. SHIFU. COACH. SPIRIT ANIMAL
...
Who is working out with you in your mind's eye? Who's your body inspiration?

THE vibe AIMED 4:

THE PLAYLIST:
1.
2.
3.
4.

Monthly workout mantra:

SUPPLEMENTS Focus:

Workout Focus:
physical therapy
fascia
somatic therapy
lymphatic
massage
rest
stabilization
strength
swimming
walking
running
endurance
dance
cardio
plyometrics
HIIT
cardio
agility
stretching
qigong
yoga
pilates

Monthly workout LOG:

MON	TUE	WED	THU	FRI	SAT	SUN	FOCUS

...the REST RIT[UAL]S:

"At least ONCE a MONTH I..."

pre | post workout drink LOG

Pick 4 Forms or styles to focus on Getting better with:

E.g.:

Yoga?

Qi Gong?

Stretching?

Swimming?

How many times a week?

How Long?

AM / PM
Intention:

Thought Prompt :

Journal Prompt

Safe word

Synchronicity you'd like to see

Miracles to be on the lookout for

Prayer Requests

sunrise dayUP Geterdone:

Sunset slow down b4BED Geterdone:

Go FI D &/or DO SOMETHING BEAUTIFUL

Curious about it? <u>Learn it</u>

Wish you were able 2 do it? <u>Try it</u>

Place you want 2go? <u>Go 2it</u>

Love to have it outside?<u>Try it @home</u>

Habit 2 improve

Habit 2 give up

Replace with what?

How ?

Accountability:

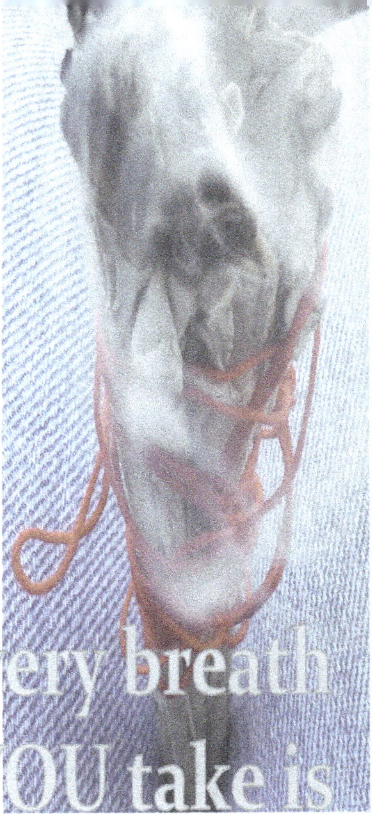

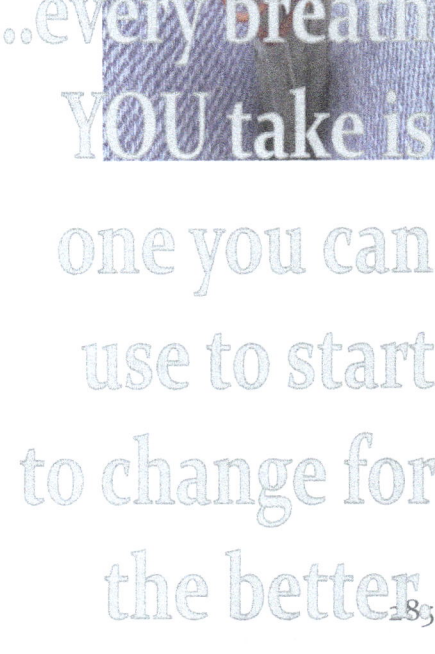

...every breath YOU take is one you can use to start to change for the better.

Theme

Year

Month

This month's HIGHEST TIMELINE log line:

Your Life's movie title:

POINT OF THE MONTH:

[NECESSARY] COUNTERPOINT OF THE MONTH:

(EVERY POINT HAS A COUNTERPOINT)

AUDIO BOOK

HAPTIC BOOK

EBOOK:

PODCAST

MOVIE

ODD INTEREST

SPIRITUAL SUBJECT

HERB | FLOWER

CRYSTAL | INCENSE

QUOTE | POET

M	T

Give yourself ONE day a week. Purely For YOU.. One way or another. Find a way.

Harvest Fall Winter Spring Summer

MAR APR MAY
JUN JUL AUG
SEP OCT NOV
DEC JAN FEB

I & I DAY
I & I HOUR:
HOLY DAYS
BIRTHDAYS etc.,.

FULL MOON
NEW MOON
CYCLE START
CYCLE END

W	T	F	S	S
			Ordered || Due	

HO ARE YOU?   HOW are YOU EXPRESSING IT?

287

Revisit, revise, release, re-adjust, re-calibrate...

Last quarter

Free Write

Themes:

Video deep dive teachers:

Full Moon

Date:

1. Cleanse your space [Mental & physical].

2. Crystals? Charge 'em!.

3. Celebrate any wins.

4. Release what no longer Serves you.

5. Get out in some moonlight.

Free Write

Themes:

Video deep dive teachers:

1st quarter

Themes:

Deep Dive Teachers:

292

Accepting abundance | Free Write

Free Write

<u>Themes:</u>

<u>Deep Dive Teachers:</u>

New Moon

Date:

1. Imagine what you aim to Bring into your zone..
2. Set new intentions.
3. Journal & Meditate.
4. Scrub &/or soak your body.
5. Get out in some moonlight.

THE MONTH of 12:

"MY BODY CAN"

(OF THE MONTH)

NOTES:

SIFU. SHIFU. COACH. SPIRIT ANIMAL
...
Who is working out with you in your mind's eye? Who's your body inspiration?

THE vibe AIMED 4:

THE PLAYLIST:
1.
2.
3.
4.

Monthy workout mantra:

SUPPLEMENTS Focus:

Workout Focus:
physical therapy
fascia
somatic therapy
lymphatic
massage
rest
stabilization
strength
swimming
walking
running
endurance
dance
cardio
plyometrics
HIIT
cardio
agility
stretching
qigong
yoga
pilates

Monthly workout LOG:

MON	TUE	WED	THU	FRI	SAT	SUN	FOCUS

...the **REST RIT**[UAL]**S:**

"At least ONCE a MONTH I..."

pre | post workout drink LOG

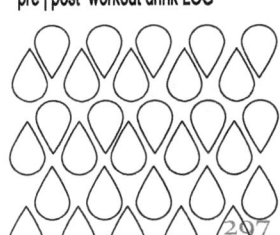

Pick 4 Forms or styles to focus on Getting better with:

E.g.:

Yoga?

Qi Gong?

Stretching?

Swimming?

How many times a week?

How Long?

AM / PM
Intention:

Thought Prompt :

Journal Prompt

Safe word

Synchronicity you'd like to see

Miracles to be on the lookout for

Prayer Requests

sunrise dayUP Geterdone:

Sunset slow down b4BED Geterdone:

Go FI_ _D &/or DO SOMETHING BEAUTIFUL

Curious about it? <u>Learn it</u>

Wish you were able 2 do it? <u>Try it</u>

Place you want 2go? <u>Go 2it</u>

Love to have it outside?<u>Try it @home</u>

Habit 2 improve

Habit 2 give up

Replace with what?

How ?

Accountability:

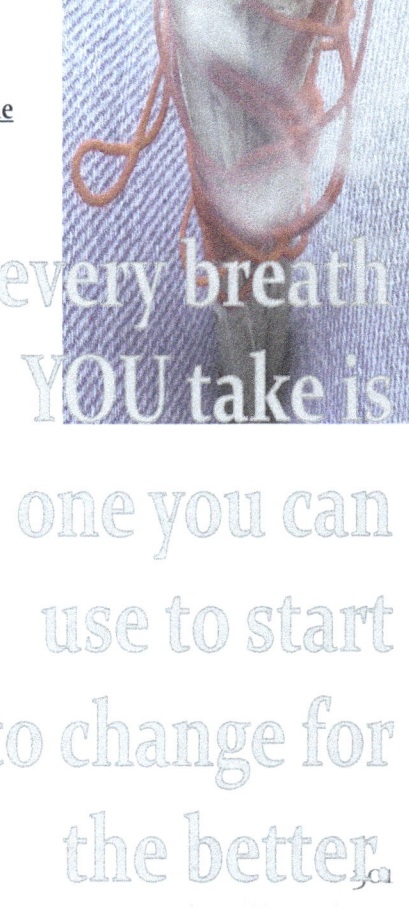

...every breath YOU take is one you can use to start to change for the better.

Theme

Year

Month

POINT OF THE MONTH:

[NECESSARY] COUNTERPOINT OF THE MONTH:

(EVERY POINT HAS A COUNTERPOINT)

AUDIO BOOK

HAPTIC BOOK

EBOOK:

PODCAST

MOVIE

ODD INTEREST

SPIRITUAL SUBJECT

HERB | FLOWER

CRYSTAL | INCENSE

QUOTE | POET

This month's HIGHEST TIMELINE log line:

Your Life's movie title:

M	T

Give yourself ONE day a week. Purely For YOU.. One way or another. Find a way.

Harvest Fall Winter Spring Summer

**MAR APR MAY
JUN JUL AUG
SEP OCT NOV
DEC JAN FEB**

I & I DAY
I & I HOUR:
HOLY DAYS
BIRTHDAYS etc.,.

FULL MOON
NEW MOON
CYCLE START
CYCLE END

W	T	F	S	S
			**Ordered		Due**	

HO ARE YOU?   **HOW are YOU EXPRESSING IT?**

303

Revisit, revise, release, re-adjust, re-calibrate...

Last quarter

Free Write

Themes:

Video deep dive teachers:

Full Moon

Date:

- 1. Cleanse your space [Mental & physical].
- 2. Crystals? Charge 'em!.
- 3. Celebrate any wins.
- 4. Release what no longer Serves you.
- 5. Get out in some moonlight.

Free Write

Themes:

Video deep dive teachers:

1st quarter

Themes:

Deep Dive Teachers:

Free Write

<u>Themes:</u>

<u>Deep Dive Teachers:</u>

New Moon

Date:

1. Imagine what you aim to Bring into your zone..

2. Set new intentions.

3. Journal & Meditate.

4. Scrub &/or soak your body.

5. Get out in some moonlight.

THE MONTH of 12:

NOTES:

"MY BODY CAN"

(OF THE MONTH)

SIFU. SHIFU. COACH. SPIRIT ANIMAL
...
Who is working out with you in your mind's eye? Who's your body inspiration?

THE vibe AIMED 4:

THE PLAYLIST:
1.
2.
3.
4.

Monthly workout mantra:

SUPPLEMENTS Focus:

Workout Focus:
physical therapy
fascia
somatic therapy
lymphatic
massage
rest
stabilization
strength
swimming
walking
running
endurance
dance
cardio
plyometrics
HIIT
cardio
agility
stretching
qigong
yoga
pilates

Monthly workout LOG:

MON	TUE	WED	THU	FRI	SAT	SUN	FOCUS

...the REST RIT[UAL]S:

"At least ONCE a MONTH I..."

pre | post workout drink LOG

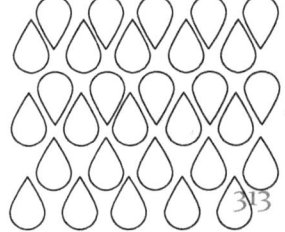

Pick 4 Forms or styles to focus on Getting better with:

E.g.:

Yoga?

Qi Gong?

Stretching?

Swimming?

How many times a week?

How Long?

AM / PM
Intention:

Thought Prompt :

Journal Prompt

Safe word

Synchronicity you'd like to see

Miracles to be on the lookout for

Prayer Requests

sunrise dayUP Geterdone:

Sunset slow down b4BED Geterdone:

Go FI D &/or DO SOMETHING BEAUTIFUL

Curious about it? <u>Learn it</u>

Wish you were able 2 do it? <u>Try it</u>

Place you want 2go? <u>Go 2it</u>

Love to have it outside?<u>Try it @home</u>

Habit 2 improve

Habit 2 give up

Replace with what?

How ?

Accountability:

...every breath YOU take is one you can use to start to change for the better.

Theme

Year

Month

POINT OF THE MONTH:

[NECESSARY] COUNTERPOINT OF THE MONTH:

(EVERY POINT HAS A COUNTERPOINT)

AUDIO BOOK

HAPTIC BOOK

EBOOK:

PODCAST

MOVIE

ODD INTEREST

SPIRITUAL SUBJECT

HERB | FLOWER

CRYSTAL | INCENSE

QUOTE | POET

This month's HIGHEST TIMELINE log line:

Your Life's movie title:

M	T

Give yourself ONE day a week. Purely For YOU.. One way or another. Find a way.

Harvest Fall Winter Spring Summer

MAR APR MAY
JUN JUL AUG
SEP OCT NOV
DEC JAN FEB

I & I DAY
I & I HOUR:
HOLY DAYS
BIRTHDAYS etc.,.

FULL MOON
NEW MOON
CYCLE START
CYCLE END

W	T	F	S	S
			Ordered ||Due	

HO ARE YOU?   **HOW are YOU EXPRESSING IT?**

Revisit, revise, release, readjust, re-calibrate...

Last quarter

Free Write

Themes:

Video deep dive teachers:

Full Moon

Date:

- 1. Cleanse your space [Mental & physical].
- 2. Crystals? Charge 'em!.
- 3. Celebrate any wins.
- 4. Release what no longer Serves you.
- 5. Get out in some moonlight.

Free Write

Themes:

Video deep dive teachers:

1st quarter

Themes:

Deep Dive Teachers:

Free Write

Themes:

Deep Dive Teachers:

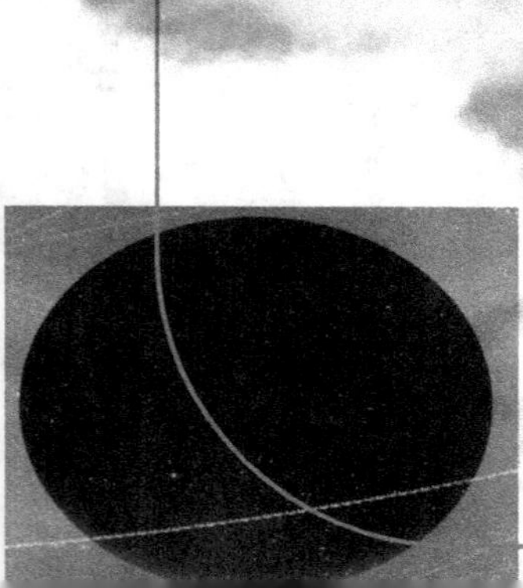

THE MONTH of 12:

NOTES:

"MY BODY CAN"

(OF THE MONTH)

SIFU. SHIFU. COACH. SPIRIT ANIMAL

...

Who is working out with you in your mind's eye? Who's your body inspiration?

THE vibe AIMED 4:

THE PLAYLIST:

1.
2.
3.
4.

Monthly workout mantra:

SUPPLEMENTS Focus:

Workout Focus:
physical therapy
fascia
somatic therapy
lymphatic
massage
rest
stabilization
strength
swimming
walking
running
endurance
dance
cardio
plyometrics
HIIT
cardio
agility
stretching
qigong
yoga
pilates

Monthly workout LOG:

MON	TUE	WED	THU	FRI	SAT	SUN	FOCUS

...the **REST RIT**[UAL]**S**:

"At least ONCE a MONTH I..."

pre | post workout drink LOG

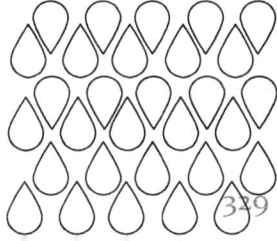

Pick 4 Forms or styles to focus on Getting better with:

E.g.:

Yoga?

Qi Gong?

Stretching?

Swimming?

How many times a week?

How Long?

AM / PM
Intention:

Thought Prompt :

Journal Prompt

Safe word

Synchronicity you'd like to see

Miracles to be on the lookout for

Prayer Requests

sunrise dayUP Geterdone:

Sunset slow down b4BED Geterdone:

Go FI D &/or DO SOMETHING BEAUTIFUL

Curious about it? <u>Learn it</u>

Wish you were able 2 do it? <u>Try it</u>

Place you want 2go? <u>Go 2it</u>

Love to have it outside?<u>Try it @home</u>

Habit 2 improve

Habit 2 give up

Replace with what?

How ?

Accountability:

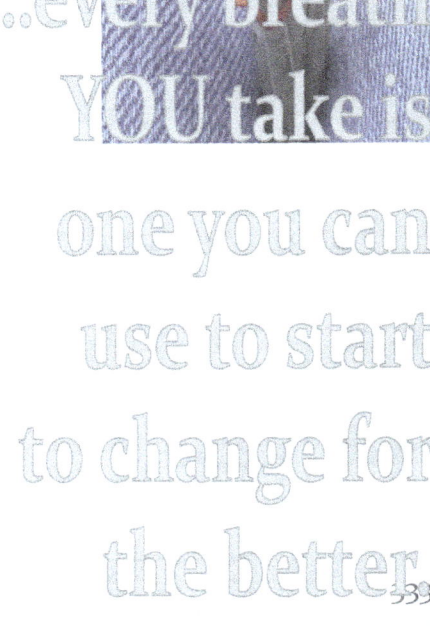

...every breath YOU take is one you can use to start to change for the better.

Theme

Year

Month

This month's HIGHEST TIMELINE log line:

Your Life's movie title:

POINT OF THE MONTH:

[NECESSARY] COUNTERPOINT OF THE MONTH:

(EVERY POINT HAS A COUNTERPOINT)

AUDIO BOOK

HAPTIC BOOK

EBOOK:

PODCAST

MOVIE

ODD INTEREST

SPIRITUAL SUBJECT

HERB | FLOWER

CRYSTAL | INCENSE

QUOTE | POET

M	T

Give yourself ONE day a week. Purely For YOU.. One way or another. Find a way.

Harvest Fall Winter Spring Summer

MAR APR MAY
JUN JUL AUG
SEP OCT NOV
DEC JAN FEB

I & I DAY
I & I HOUR:
HOLY DAYS
BIRTHDAYS etc.,.

FULL MOON
NEW MOON
CYCLE START
CYCLE END

W	T	F	S	S
			Ordered | | Due	

WHO ARE YOU?   HOW are YOU EXPRESSING IT?

Revisit, revise, release, readjust, recalibrate...

Last quarter

Free Write

Themes:

Video deep dive teachers:

Full Moon

Date:

- 1. Cleanse your space [Mental & physical].
- 2. Crystals? Charge 'em!.
- 3. Celebrate any wins.
- 4. Release what no longer Serves you.
- 5. Get out in some moonlight.

Free Write

Themes:

Video deep dive teachers:

1st quarter

Themes:

Deep Dive Teachers:

Accepting abundance | Free Write

Free Write

Themes:

Deep Dive Teachers:

THE MONTH of 12:

NOTES:

"MY BODY CAN"

(OF THE MONTH)

SIFU. SHIFU. COACH. SPIRIT ANIMAL
...
Who is working out with you in your mind's eye? Who's your body inspiration?

THE vibe AIMED 4:

THE PLAYLIST:
1.
2.
3.
4.

Monthly workout mantra:

SUPPLEMENTS Focus:

Workout Focus:
physical therapy
fascia
somatic therapy
lymphatic
massage
rest
stabilization
strength
swimming
walking
running
endurance
dance
cardio
plyometrics
HIIT
cardio
agility
stretching
qigong
yoga
pilates

Monthly workout LOG:

MON	TUE	WED	THU	FRI	SAT	SUN	FOCUS

...the REST RIT[UAL]S:

"At least ONCE a MONTH I..."

pre | post workout drink LOG

Pick 4 Forms or styles to focus on Getting better with:

E.g.:

Yoga?

Qi Gong?

Stretching?

Swimming?

How many times a week?

How Long?

AM / PM
Intention:

Thought Prompt :

Journal Prompt

Safe word

Synchronicity you'd like to see

Miracles to be on the lookout for

Prayer Requests

sunrise dayUP Geterdone:

Sunset slow down b4BED Geterdone:

Go FI D &/or DO SOMETHING BEAUTIFUL

Curious about it? <u>Learn it</u>

Wish you were able 2 do it? <u>Try it</u>

Place you want 2go? <u>Go 2it</u>

Love to have it outside?<u>Try it @home</u>

Habit 2 improve

Habit 2 give up

Replace with what?

How ?

Accountability:

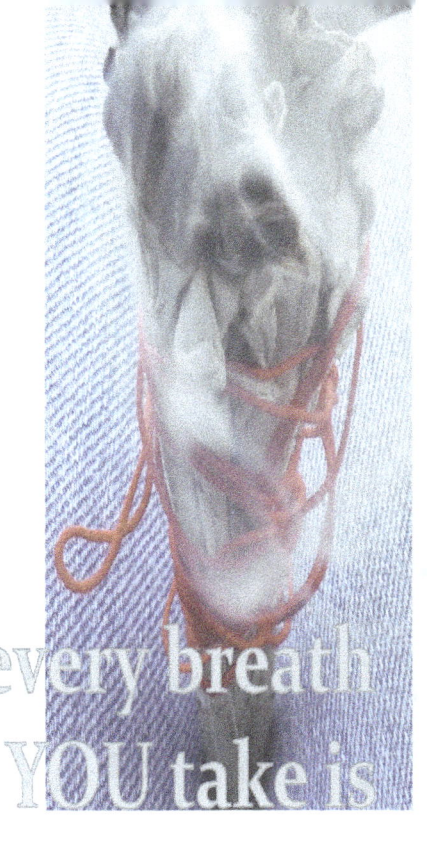

...every breath YOU take is one you can use to start to change for the better.

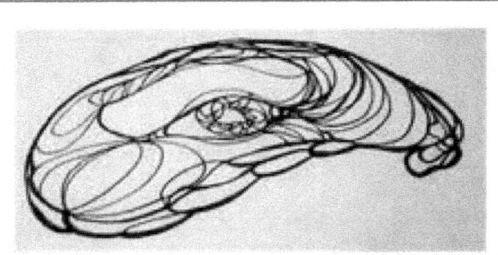

angel brynner.

KOKOPELLIMA PRESS

www.ingramcontent.com/pod-product-compliance
Lightning Source LLC
Chambersburg PA
CBHW070126080526
44586CB00015B/1578